opendoors

REPORT ON INTERNATIONAL EDUCATIONAL EXCHANGE

Hey-Kyung Koh Chin, Editor
Senior Program Officer

With Adria Gallup-Black, Ph.D.
Director of Research & Evaluation

Institute of International Education

D1316633

CONTENTS

OPEN DOORS is a long-standing, comprehensive information resource on nearly 573,000 international students in the United States in 2003/04 and on the almost 175,000 U.S. students who studied abroad for academic credit in 2002/03. The Institute of International Education, the largest and most experienced U.S. higher education exchange agency, has conducted an annual statistical survey of the internationally mobile student population in the United States since 1948, with U.S. government support since 1972.

Suggested Citation: *Open Doors 2004: Report on International Educational Exchange*, 2004. Hey-Kyung Koh Chin, ed. New York: Institute of International Education.

The boundaries and other information shown on any map, or referenced in text or in any figure or table in this volume, do not imply any judgment on the legal status of any territory or the endorsement or acceptance of such boundaries by the Institute of International Education, Inc. or any instrumentality of the United States Government.

572,509 international students were studying at U.S. campuses in 2003/04, a decline of 2.4%.

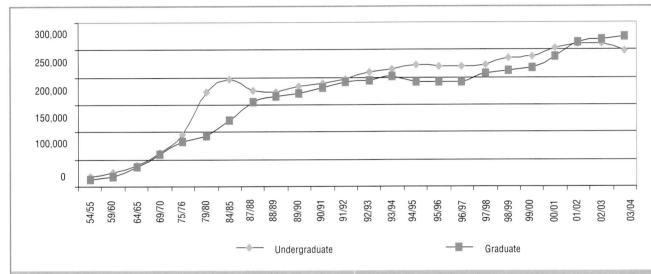

International undergraduates have long outnumbered graduates, but a reversal in international enrollment by academic level began in 2001/02.

Academic Level	Int'l Students	Total U.S. Students*	% of U.S. Enrollment
Associate's	69,541	4,380,618	1.6
Bachelor's	178,659	7,109,199	2.5
Graduate**	274,310	1,893,736	14.5
Total	**572,509**	**13,383,553**	**4.3**

The ratio of international to all U.S. higher education students was over three times greater for graduate students than for undergraduate students.

* College Board Annual Survey of Colleges data on U.S. higher education enrollment

** Includes first professional degrees

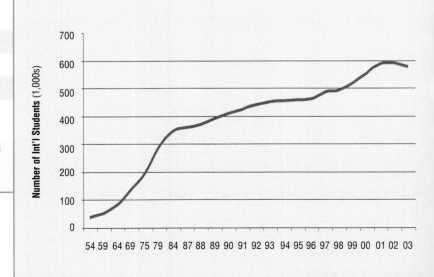

Periods of steep growth in international students have been followed by periods of minimal growth, with significant growth from 1998 to 2001.

Year	Int'l Students	Annual % Change	Total Enrollment *	% Int'l
1954/55	34,232	-	2,499,800	1.4
1959/60	48,486	2.6	3,402,300	1.4
1964/65	82,045	9.7	5,320,000	1.5
1969/70	134,959	11.2	7,978,400	1.7
1974/75	154,580	2.3	10,321,500	1.5
1979/80	286,343	8.5	11,707,000	2.4
1984/85	342,113	0.9	12,467,700	2.7
1985/86	343,777	0.5	12,387,700	2.8
1986/87	349,609	1.7	12,410,500	2.8
1987/88	356,187	1.9	12,808,487	2.8
1988/89	366,354	2.9	13,322,576	2.7
1989/90	386,851	5.6	13,824,592	2.8
1990/91	407,529	5.3	13,975,408	2.9
1991/92	419,585	3.0	14,360,965	2.9
1992/93	438,618	4.5	14,422,975	3.0
1993/94	449,749	2.5	14,473,106	3.1
1994/95	452,653	0.6	14,554,016	3.1
1995/96	453,787	0.3	14,419,252	3.1
1996/97	457,984	0.9	14,286,478	3.1
1997/98	481,280	5.1	13,294,221 **	3.6
1998/99	490,933	2.0	13,391,401	3.6
1999/00	514,723	4.8	13,584,998	3.8
2000/01	547,867	6.4	14,046,659	3.9
2001/02	582,996	6.4	13,511,149	4.3
2002/03	586,323	0.6	12,853,627	4.6
2003/04	572,509	-2.4	13,383,553	4.3

The number of international students has risen sharply since 1954, but still represents just over 4% of total U.S. higher education enrollment.

*   College Board Annual Survey of Colleges data on U.S. higher education enrollment

** In 1997, the College Board changed its data collection process.

THE BIG PICTURE

The 2003/04 academic year marked, for the first time in over 30 years, a decline in the number of international students, and only the second such decline since 1954/55, when the Institute of International Education began collecting data on international students systematically and reporting those findings in the *Open Doors Report on International Educational Exchange*.

There was a mix of factors behind the decline, including the post-September 11 security-related changes in visa policy that generated perceptions abroad that the United States is closing its doors to international students and scholars; the increasing cost of higher education in the U.S.; the growth of home countries' capacity to provide quality higher educational opportunities; and competition from other host countries.

The emerging story within this decline was quite complex: while undergraduate enrollments declined by 5%, graduate enrollments increased by 2.4%. The sharp drop in undergraduate enrollments began in 2001/02, but may have been accelerated by parental concerns about whether the U.S. is a safe and welcoming place. The modest gains in graduate enrollments were largely at smaller institutions, including those granting mainly master's and professional degrees. At the same time, the large research institutions suffered losses at the graduate level: although the overall percentage declines were small (less than 1%), the impact was great because these types of institutions serve the largest percentage (approximately 70%) of international graduate students [see p. 13].

International education

$13 billion to the

State	Int'l Students 2003/04	Tuition & Fees[1] 2003/04	Living Exp. & Dependents[2] 2003/04	Less U.S. Support[3] 2003/04	Total Contribution 2003/04	State	Int'l Students 2003/04	Tuition & Fees[1] 2003/04	Living Exp. & Dependents[2] 2003/04	Less U.S. Support[3] 2003/04	Total Contribution 2003/04
Alabama	6,386	49,729,588	89,138,321	41,493,690	97,374,219	Montana	872	8,589,832	14,556,997	5,085,515	18,061,313
Alaska	427	3,496,515	7,564,724	3,687,236	7,374,003	Nebraska	3,524	31,006,627	57,603,324	22,060,131	66,549,820
Arizona	9,907	94,049,499	170,844,016	69,643,454	195,250,061	Nevada	2,743	21,096,400	52,908,235	14,020,373	59,984,262
Arkansas	2,781	24,516,691	43,559,385	19,793,998	48,282,077	New Hampshire	2,128	32,281,619	46,095,666	18,140,908	60,236,378
California	77,186	955,231,094	1,402,284,479	551,287,776	1,806,227,797	New Jersey	13,163	153,657,668	238,876,541	98,416,135	294,118,074
Colorado	5,960	89,275,536	108,250,909	61,038,912	136,487,533	New Mexico	2,115	20,620,044	40,155,498	20,269,813	40,505,728
Connecticut	7,655	129,294,743	163,394,279	93,949,339	198,739,683	New York	63,313	938,637,361	1,218,420,495	569,470,512	1,587,587,345
Delaware	2,142	25,457,957	35,644,915	16,329,865	44,773,008	North Carolina	8,826	130,633,859	160,714,500	96,214,579	195,133,780
D.C.	8,532	150,682,777	182,317,493	103,542,765	229,457,504	North Dakota	1,595	11,838,037	24,618,348	8,131,075	28,325,311
Florida	25,861	302,303,125	465,341,735	183,039,495	584,605,365	Ohio	18,770	267,472,147	374,237,626	212,160,326	429,549,447
Georgia	12,010	149,265,898	205,900,878	100,361,102	254,805,673	Oklahoma	8,764	69,073,670	153,783,411	54,739,564	168,117,518
Guam	69	387,990	879,248	132,603	1,134,635	Oregon	5,855	73,617,803	100,706,281	44,080,548	130,243,536
Hawaii	5,371	41,246,654	97,849,584	34,867,366	104,228,871	Pennsylvania	23,428	432,659,771	464,621,866	267,197,379	630,084,258
Idaho	1,727	14,371,330	30,637,852	10,785,905	34,223,277	Puerto Rico	876	3,370,469	15,244,483	7,025,067	11,589,884
Illinois	25,609	373,530,957	526,336,575	309,296,297	590,571,235	Rhode Island	3,337	56,255,703	59,943,997	27,921,217	88,278,483
Indiana	13,586	204,650,494	272,048,148	146,716,614	329,982,028	South Carolina	3,919	43,292,634	73,727,831	40,391,753	76,628,712
Iowa	7,699	96,186,884	147,440,972	79,385,661	164,242,195	South Dakota	715	5,402,669	9,825,867	5,005,970	10,222,565
Kansas	6,573	53,226,055	105,150,635	39,830,770	118,545,920	Tennessee	5,846	77,002,577	94,357,807	57,084,566	114,275,818
Kentucky	4,751	43,818,403	69,377,749	31,800,265	81,395,888	Texas	45,150	366,875,294	738,269,198	295,260,452	809,884,040
Louisiana	6,621	72,593,059	113,999,786	54,393,774	132,199,071	Utah	5,781	34,467,084	102,095,123	34,125,500	102,436,707
Maine	1,730	20,432,422	27,923,783	16,236,156	32,120,050	Vermont	835	14,076,652	13,958,773	8,424,395	19,611,030
Maryland	12,633	155,508,966	240,349,159	108,009,357	287,848,768	Virginia	12,531	146,975,377	201,803,780	92,768,460	256,010,698
Massachusetts	28,634	559,051,051	656,854,233	371,638,798	844,266,487	Washington	10,756	119,128,045	180,674,123	62,862,286	236,939,883
Michigan	22,277	280,696,599	358,332,721	190,606,919	448,422,401	West Virginia	2,507	24,121,212	44,852,631	22,929,062	46,044,781
Minnesota	9,143	109,654,338	151,460,516	77,310,376	183,804,478	Wisconsin	7,142	121,382,051	122,063,407	79,162,980	164,282,478
Mississippi	2,280	18,562,300	35,591,574	19,494,462	34,659,411	Wyoming	493	3,362,855	8,830,814	3,668,338	8,525,331
Missouri	9,975	136,565,472	179,195,438	86,809,550	228,951,360	**Totals**	**572,509**	**7,360,683,,857**	**10,500,615,728**	**4,988,099,408**	**12,873,200,177**

International students in the U.S. made a considerable contribution to the economy through tuition payments and cost of living expenditures.

1. 2003/04 tuition, living, miscellaneous expenses from the College Board. These expenses are computed separately for undergraduate and graduate students and the sum of the two groups is reported here.
2. See p. 55 for *Open Doors* estimate of percent of international students who are married. The number of spouses in the U.S. is approximated at 85% of the number of married students. The number of children is estimated to be six for every ten couples in the U.S. The presence of a spouse increases living expenses by 25%. The presence of a child increases living expenses by 20%.
3. U.S. funding support level is computed based on the institution's Carnegie Type.
Analysis prepared for NAFSA: Association of International Educators by Jason Baumgartner and Lynn Schoch of Indiana University – Bloomington, using enrollment data from the Open Doors 2003/04 International Student Census.

contributed nearly
U.S. economy.

FINANCIAL CONTRIBUTIONS

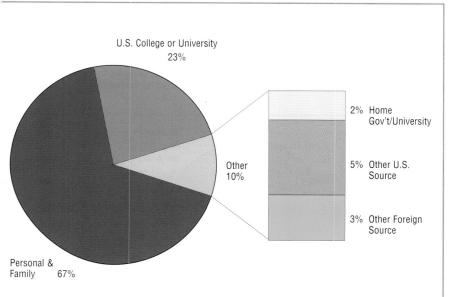

U.S. College or University
23%

2% Home Gov't/University

Other 10%

5% Other U.S. Source

3% Other Foreign Source

Personal & Family 67%

Over two-thirds of international students funded their U.S. studies primarily with personal & family funds.

Primary Source of Funds	All Int'l Students	% Under-graduate	% Graduate	% Other
Personal & Family	67.3	81.7	51.4	69.7
U.S. College or University	23.4	10.2	40.5	7.8
Home Government/University	2.4	2.0	2.2	4.1
U.S. Government	0.5	0.3	0.7	0.3
U.S. Private Sponsor	2.2	2.8	1.5	2.0
Foreign Private Sponsor	2.1	2.6	1.7	1.3
International Organization	0.3	0.2	0.5	0.8
Current Employment	1.8	0.3	1.4	13.9
Other	0.0	0.0	0.0	0.0
Total	**572,509**	**248,200**	**274,310**	**49,999**

Slightly over half of international graduate students relied on personal and family funds to finance their U.S. education, as compared to over 80% of international undergraduate students.

International students contribute not only to academic discourse and student life on U.S. campuses, but also to the U.S. national and local economies. In 2003/04, international students contributed almost $13 billion to the U.S. economy, according to analyses conducted by researchers at Indiana University for NAFSA: Association of International Educators. Expenditures include tuition, cost of living expenses, and for some, expenditures for dependents, who often stay with the students for the duration of their studies.

International students used a variety of funding sources for their U.S. higher education. In 2003/04, over two-thirds of international students (67%) relied primarily on personal and family funds. International undergraduate students generally are more dependent than graduate students upon this support source. The percentage of undergraduates relying upon personal and family funds increased from 78% in 2002/03 to 82% in 2003/04, while the percentage for graduate students remained virtually unchanged. International graduate students, especially those at large research institutions, tend to have more U.S.-based sources of funding, mostly from U.S. colleges and universities in the form of research grants and teaching assistantships (many of which are federally-supported). Only about 5% of international students received their primary funding from international sources, which include home governments and universities, and private sponsors.

India was the leading plac
with a 7% increase from

Rank	Place of Origin	2002/03	2003/04	2003/04 % Change	% of Int'l Student Total
WORLD TOTAL		**586,323**	**572,509**	**-2.4**	
1	India	74,603	79,736	6.9	13.9
2	China	64,757	61,765	-4.6	10.8
3	Korea, Republic of	51,519	52,484	1.9	9.2
4	Japan	45,960	40,835	-11.2	7.1
5	Canada	26,513	27,017	1.9	4.7
6	Taiwan	28,017	26,178	-6.6	4.6
7	Mexico	12,801	13,329	4.1	2.3
8	Turkey	11,601	11,398	-1.7	2.0
9	Thailand	9,982	8,937	-10.5	1.6
10	Indonesia	10,432	8,880	-14.9	1.6
11	Germany	9,302	8,745	-6.0	1.5
12	United Kingdom	8,326	8,439	1.4	1.5
13	Brazil	8,388	7,799	-7.0	1.4
14	Colombia	7,771	7,533	-3.1	1.3
15	Kenya	7,862	7,381	-6.1	1.3
16	Hong Kong	8,076	7,353	-9.0	1.3
17	Pakistan	8,123	7,325	-9.8	1.3
18	France	7,223	6,818	-5.6	1.2
19	Malaysia	6,595	6,483	-1.7	1.1
20	Nigeria	5,816	6,140	5.6	1.1

The leading four places of origin, all of which are in Asia, represented 41% of international students in the U.S.

of origin,
the previous year.

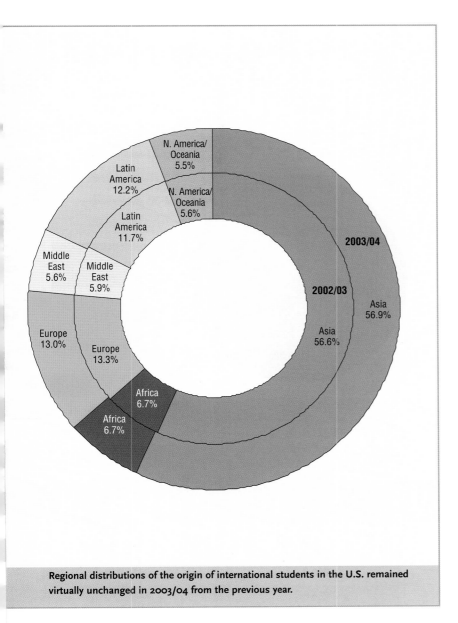

N. America/
Oceania
5.5%

Latin
America
12.2%

N. America/
Oceania
5.6%

Latin
America
11.7%

2003/04

Middle
East
5.6%

Middle
East
5.9%

2002/03

Asia
56.9%

Europe
13.0%

Europe
13.3%

Asia
56.6%

Africa
6.7%

Africa
6.7%

Regional distributions of the origin of international students in the U.S. remained virtually unchanged in 2003/04 from the previous year.

THEIR ORIGINS

For the third consecutive year, India was the leading place of origin of international students at U.S. campuses. A total of 79,736 Indian students studied in the U.S. in 2003/04; however, the increase from the prior year was only 7%, which is a drop from the double-digit increases seen in the prior two years (12% in 2002/03 and 22% in 2001/02). Among the top five sending places of origin, India, China, the Republic of Korea, and Japan maintained their respective positions from last year. The only change was in the fifth position, in which Canada replaced Taiwan (which dropped to sixth place).

Among the top 20 sending places of origin, there were more declines than increases. The number of students from China declined almost 5% from the previous year, to 61,765. Enrollments from Japan fell by 11%, to 40,835. Other declines ranged from less than 2% for Turkey and Malaysia to almost 15% for Indonesia. The increases among the top 20 senders were generally smaller than the declines, ranging from 7% for India and 6% for Nigeria to just over 1% for the United Kingdom.

While the overall number of international students declined by 2.4%, the regional distribution of international students in 2003/04 was almost identical to that seen the previous year. Any differences from 2002/03 were within 1%. Students from Asia continued to comprise about 57% of the total international student population.

with adjacent communities having a high degree of economic and social integration with that core.

Almost half of all international students were located in just 20 metropolitan areas.

The number of international students in the top three fields of study – business & management, engineering, and mathematics & computer sciences – declined 4% from the previous year.

Year	% Male	% Single	% F Visa	Int'l Students
1977/78	75.0	77.4	78.8	235,509
1978/79	74.1	74.7	80.7	263,938
1979/80	72.4	78.6	82.0	286,343
1980/81	71.7	80.1	82.9	311,882
1981/82	71.0	79.3	84.3	326,299
1982/83	70.9	80.1	84.0	336,985
1983/84	70.6	80.1	83.2	338,894
1984/85	69.8	80.4	83.5	342,113
1985/86	70.7	80.0	81.5	343,777
1986/87	68.9	79.7	81.0	349,609
1987/88	67.7	79.8	79.4	356,187
1988/89	66.5	80.9	79.0	366,354
1989/90	66.1	80.1	78.5	386,851
1990/91	64.0	78.5	80.6	407,529
1991/92	63.7	80.7	84.6	419,585
1992/93	63.0	82.5	85.5	438,618
1993/94	62.1	83.1	86.4	449,749
1994/95	60.9	83.4	85.8	452,635
1995/96	58.9	82.6	84.9	453,787
1996/97	59.0	84.4	85.6	457,984
1997/98	58.1	83.6	86.8	481,280
1998/99	58.0	85.2	87.3	490,933
1999/00	57.5	84.2	85.6	514,723
2000/01	57.1	84.7	85.8	547,867
2001/02	57.0	86.0	86.2	582,996
2002/03	56.2	85.0	86.0	586,323
2003/04	55.8	85.3	85.7	572,509

Despite steady increases in the numbers of female international students since 1977, the typical profile of an international student remained a single male on an F Visa.

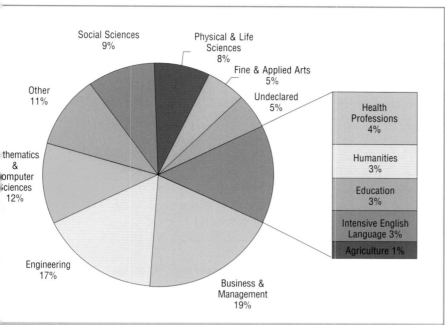

Business & management remained the most popular field of study among international students, followed by engineering.

Field of Study	2002/03 Int'l Students	2003/04 Int'l Students	% of Total	% Change
TOTAL	**586,323**	**572,509**	**100.0**	**-2.4**
Business & Management	114,777	109,187	19.1	-4.9
Engineering	96,545	95,183	16.6	-1.4
Mathematics & Computer Sciences	71,926	67,736	11.8	-5.8
Other	58,473	60,212	10.5	3.0
Social Sciences	45,978	54,083	9.4	17.6
Physical & Life Sciences	43,549	44,605	7.8	2.4
Fine & Applied Arts	31,018	31,817	5.6	2.6
Undeclared	36,395	29,265	5.1	-19.6
Health Professions	28,120	25,693	4.5	-8.6
Humanities	19,153	16,593	2.9	-13.4
Education	16,004	15,888	2.8	-0.7
Intensive English Language	17,620	14,971	2.6	-15.0
Agriculture	6,763	7,276	1.3	7.6

The three most popular fields of study among international students – business and management, engineering, and mathematics and computer sciences – all experienced declines in 2003/04.

FIELDS OF STUDY

International students pursue a full range of fields of study, but in 2003/04 nearly half (48%) were in three fields of study: business and management, engineering, and mathematics and computer sciences. The leading field of study remained business and management, with 109,187, or 19% of all international students. Engineering, with 95,183 students, comprised almost 17% of the total, followed by mathematics and computer sciences, with 67,736 students, almost 12% of the total. All three fields saw declines (-5%, -1%, and -6%, respectively) for a combined decline of 4%.

Unlike the field of study changes over time, some characteristics of international students studying in the U.S. have remained fairly consistent. For example, the vast majority of international students who came to study in the U.S. were single (85%), as has been the case since the beginning of the Census. Similarly, a sizeable proportion (86%) of international students came to the U.S. to study on an F Visa. In 1977/78, three-quarters of all international students were male, but the gender gap has been closing steadily since then, with females now comprising almost half (44%) of all international students.

174,629 U.S. students studied abroad in 2002/03, an increase of 8.5% from the previous year.

Rank	Destination	2001/02	2002/03	% Change	% of all Study Abroad
	TOTAL	160,920	174,629	8.5	
1	United Kingdom	30,143	31,706	5.2	18.2
2	Italy	17,169	18,936	10.3	10.8
3	Spain	17,176	18,865	9.8	10.8
4	France	12,274	13,080	6.6	7.5
5	Australia	9,456	10,691	13.1	6.1
6	Mexico	8,078	8,775	8.6	5.0
7	Germany	4,856	5,587	15.1	3.2
8	Ireland	4,375	4,892	11.8	2.8
9	Costa Rica	3,781	4,296	13.6	2.5
10	Japan	3,168	3,457	9.1	2.0
11	Austria	2,180	2,798	28.3	1.6
12	China	3,911	2,493	-36.3	1.4
13	Greece	1,856	2,011	8.4	1.2
14	Czech Republic	1,659	1,997	20.4	1.1
15	Chile	1,492	1,944	30.3	1.1
16	New Zealand	1,326	1,917	44.6	1.1
17	Netherlands	1,676	1,792	6.9	1.0
18	South Africa	1,456	1,594	9.5	0.9
19	Ecuador	1,425	1,567	10.0	0.9
20	Russia	1,269	1,521	19.9	0.9

The choice of study abroad destinations continued to become more diverse: of the top 20 destinations, 11 were outside of Western Europe.

U.S. STUDY ABROAD

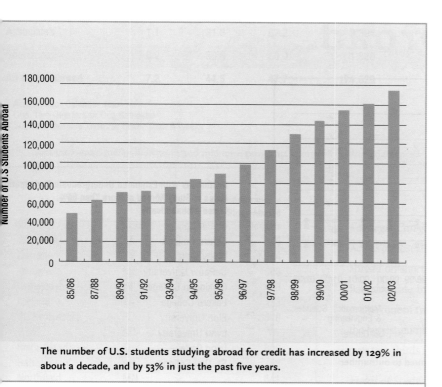

The number of U.S. students studying abroad for credit has increased by 129% in about a decade, and by 53% in just the past five years.

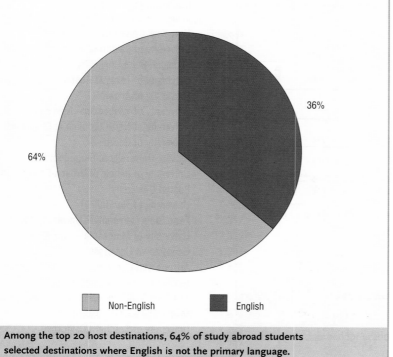

Among the top 20 host destinations, 64% of study abroad students selected destinations where English is not the primary language.

More than ever, U.S. students value an international education experience. In a world of expanding global economies, these students realize the "value added" of study abroad and incorporate it into their higher education studies. U.S. participation in study abroad for academic credit has consistently increased since 1985/86, with particularly dramatic growth since the mid-1990s. U.S. study abroad increased by 129% in about a decade, and by 53% in the past five years alone. After three years of double-digit rates of increase since 1993/94 and somewhat slower growth (4.4%) in 2001/02, the number of U.S. students abroad increased 8.5% in 2002/03 and reached an all-time high of almost 175,000 students.

Nearly half, or 47% of students, chose to study in the leading four destinations in 2002/03: U.K., Italy, Spain, and France. While Western Europe continued to be the leading host region, the percentage of U.S. students abroad in Europe has declined since the mid-1980s. Study abroad to Oceania has seen the largest percentage increase, fueled mainly by study in Australia, which has seen huge increases in recent years. Almost all of the top 20 destinations saw increases – some in the double-digits – in U.S. students in 2002/03. The exception was China, the only leading destination with a decline (37%), likely related to program cancellations and concerns resulting from the SARS outbreak in early 2003.

Although almost a quarter of U.S. students were studying in the two largest English-speaking destinations, the U.K. and Australia, 64% of the students in the top 20 destinations went to countries where English is not the primary language. More than half of the top 20 destinations were outside of Western Europe.

43,003 international students
IEPs in the U.S. in 2003, a
the previous year and a drop
of almost 50% since 2000.

Rank	Place of Origin	2002 Total Students	2003 Total Students	% of IEP Total Students	% Change	2003 Student-Weeks
	WORLD TOTAL	**51,179**	**43,003**			**495,939**
1	Japan	13,047	10,519	24.5	-19.4	122,084
2	Korea, Republic of	10,000	10,412	24.2	4.1	132,965
3	Taiwan	5,919	4,235	9.8	-28.5	52,707
4	Italy	1,171	1,408	3.3	20.2	8,034
5	Brazil	2,363	1,359	3.2	-42.5	11,782
6	France	1,231	1,156	2.7	-6.1	10,231
7	Turkey	1,102	1,034	2.4	-6.2	12,408
8	Thailand	1,245	943	2.2	-24.3	12,899
9	Mexico	936	883	2.1	-5.7	8,942
10	Colombia	1,089	858	2.0	-21.2	10,850
11	Germany	1,199	849	2.0	-29.2	7,266
12	China	1,048	796	1.9	-24.0	9,276
13	Venezuela	1,216	742	1.7	-39.0	8,800
14	Switzerland	1,564	732	1.7	-53.2	6,577
15	Spain	539	728	1.7	35.1	6,200
16	Saudi Arabia	756	348	0.8	-54.0	5,466
17	Chile	330	344	0.8	4.2	3,076
18	Ecuador	234	298	0.7	27.4	3,699
19	Russia	292	273	0.6	-6.5	2,894
20	Peru	298	269	0.6	-9.7	3,218

Almost 60% of IEP students came from the leading three places of origin, which are in Asia.

were enrolled in

16% decline from

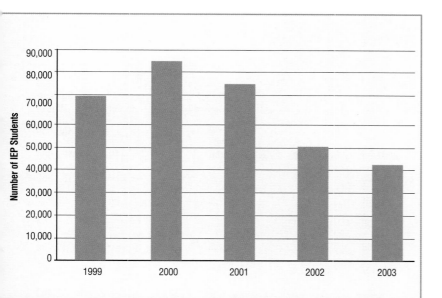

IEP enrollments have declined almost 50% since 2000.

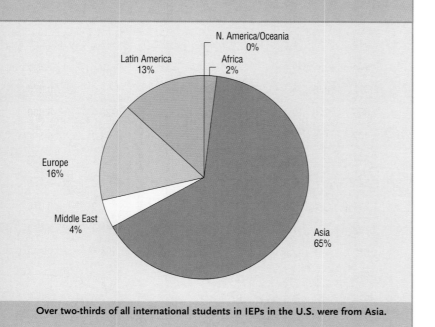

Over two-thirds of all international students in IEPs in the U.S. were from Asia.

INTENSIVE ENGLISH

A fter a decade of substantial growth, international student enrollment in Intensive English Programs (IEPs) continued its third consecutive year of declines since reaching 85,238 in 2000. The 43,003 international IEP enrollments in calendar year 2003 represent a 16% decline from the previous year and an almost 50% decline since 2000. Even more than international enrollments in degree programs, enrollments in IEPs have been sensitive to external factors, such as the events of September 11, related security concerns and subsequent changes in visa procedures, and global economic conditions.

Nearly two-thirds (65%) of all IEP students in the U.S. were from Asia, followed by Europe (slightly under 16%), and Latin America (13%). The top three places of origin – Japan, Korea, and Taiwan – comprised almost 60% of all IEP enrollments. There were double-digit declines among half of the top 20 places of origin, with the largest percentage declines found for students from Brazil, Saudi Arabia, and Switzerland. In 2003, Japan was the leading place of origin by total students (10,519), but Korea was the leading place of origin by total number of student-weeks (132,963).

The IEP survey captures data on international students enrolled in IEPs during the calendar year beginning January 1, 2003 and ending December 31, 2003. The data are collected and reported both by total headcount enrollment, as well as by student-weeks. A "student-week" is one student studying for one week. These two variables capture both student numbers, as well as their length of study, which can vary widely by program and place of origin.

82,905 international scholars were in the U.S. in 2003/04, a 1.6% decline from the previous year.

Rank	Place of Origin	2002/03	2003/04	% Change	% of U.S. Int'l Scholar Total
	WORLD TOTAL	**84,281**	**82,905**	**-1.6**	
1	China	15,206	14,871	-2.2	17.9
2	Korea, Republic of	7,286	7,290	0.1	8.8
3	India	6,565	6,809	3.7	8.2
4	Japan	5,706	5,627	-1.4	6.8
5	Germany	4,648	4,737	1.9	5.7
6	Canada	4,222	4,125	-2.3	5.0
7	United Kingdom	3,113	3,117	0.1	3.8
8	France	2,789	2,842	1.9	3.4
9	Russia	2,814	2,403	-14.6	2.9
10	Italy	2,242	2,317	3.3	2.8
11	Spain	1,717	1,893	10.3	2.3
12	Israel	1,290	1,409	9.2	1.7
13	Taiwan	1,241	1,347	8.5	1.6
14	Brazil	1,458	1,341	-8.0	1.6
15	Turkey	1,171	1,215	3.8	1.5
16	Australia	1,183	1,197	1.2	1.4
17	Mexico	1,185	1,032	-12.9	1.2
18	Netherlands	955	975	2.1	1.2
19	Poland	872	927	6.3	1.1
20	Argentina	922	820	-11.1	1.0

Nearly 18% of all international scholars in the U.S. came from China.

Number of International Scholars

100,000
90,000
80,000
70,000
60,000
50,000
40,000
30,000
20,000
10,000
0

93/94

INTERNATIONAL SCHOLARS

Leading Fields of Specialization	% of Scholars
Life & Biological Sciences	23.2
Health Sciences	20.8
Physical Sciences	13.2
Engineering	10.7
Business & Management	3.8
Computer & Information Sciences	3.7
Social Sciences & History	3.3
Agriculture	3.1
Mathematics	2.4
Other	2.2
All Others	13.8
TOTAL	**82,905**

The sciences and engineering were the leading fields of specialization of 68% of international scholars in the U.S.

96/97   97/98   98/99   99/00   00/01   01/02   02/03   03/04

After a steady increase beginning in 1994/95, the number of international scholars in the U.S. began to decline after 2001/02.

After six years of growth, the number of international scholars who were conducting research or teaching at U.S. higher education institutions declined for the second consecutive year. In 2003/04, 82,905 scholars were in the U.S., representing a 1.6% decline from 2002/03, and a 3.6% decline since 2001/02.

International scholars from the top 20 places of origin comprised 66,294, or 80%, of all scholars. In 2003/04, there were declines in the number of scholars at U.S. campuses from seven of these 20 places of origin. More European places of origin (eight) were found among the top 20 than any other region, representing about 23% of all scholars. However, the top four places of origin were in Asia, the largest sending region. Scholars from Asia made up the largest proportion of those from the top 20 places of origin (35,944), representing about 43% of all scholars. The leading place of origin in 2003/04 remained China, albeit with a 2% decline. Scholars from Spain had a double-digit increase (over 10%), while scholars from Russia, Mexico, and Argentina saw double-digit declines of approximately 15%, 13%, and 11%, respectively.

Over three-quarters of international scholars in the U.S. conducted research in their fields of specialization, while smaller percentages taught (13%), or did both research and teaching (6%). Consistent with previous years, the sciences (life and biological sciences, health sciences, physical sciences) and engineering dominated the leading fields of specialization.

Global Competition:
Other Host Countries' Expanding Share of Internationally Mobile Students

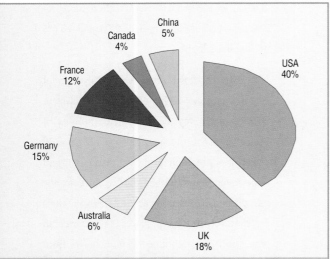

Among selected leading destinations of internationally mobile students, the United States remained dominant in 2002/03.

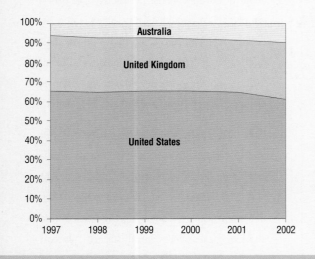

The United States' market share of international students among the leading three Anglophone host countries has declined since 1997.

The United States' market share of international students has declined since 1997, as compared with the other two largest English-speaking hosts: Australia and the United Kingdom. These two large competitors have articulated national strategies for recruiting international students, and developed coordinated campaigns abroad. Moreover, the scope of the competition is growing. While university capacity in the U.K. and Australia is limited, other countries have higher education seats to spare, particularly Japan and Germany. With strong financial incentives, geo-political motives, and need for immigrant labor in high-tech areas, other countries are also competing more vigorously and with growing support from their national governments. In addition, newly emerging hosts, such as China and India, continue to expand higher education capacity at home while also sending large numbers abroad. Thus, while the U.S. has maintained its position as the leading destination for international students, trends indicate that its lead is shrinking.

To track these trends, IIE launched the Atlas Project in 2001, as a complement to the annual *Open Doors* survey, to collect data from other major host countries. With generous funding from the Ford Foundation, this project examined the broader implications of international student mobility within a global context. In 2003, IIE published the *Atlas of Student Mobility,* which contains baseline data on worldwide student flows for the 2000/01 academic year. Since then, the project has expanded, gathering more current data from a wider cohort of countries. An *Atlas* website will be launched in early 2005, containing up-to-date data, relevant articles, and opportunities for researchers and other stakeholders to discuss critical issues pertaining to international student mobility.

A description of the *Atlas* publication and its contents, as well as the link to the *Atlas* website when it becomes available, can be found on *www.iienetwork.org.* Copies of the 2003 *Atlas* can be purchased online at *www.iiebooks.org.*

INTERNATIONAL STUDENTS

IN THIS SECTION

Place of Origin	2002/03	2003/04	% Change
AFRICA	**40,193**	**38,150**	**-5.1**
Africa, Unspecified	1	1	0.0
East Africa	**15,996**	**14,831**	**-7.3**
Burundi	66	80	21.2
Comoros	31	22	-29.0
Djibouti	5	2	-60.0
Eritrea	141	127	-9.9
Ethiopia	1,119	1,060	-5.3
Kenya	7,862	7,381	-6.1
Madagascar	119	109	-8.4
Malawi	391	399	2.0
Mauritius	228	209	-8.3
Mozambique	108	93	-13.9
Reunion	4	2	-50.0
Rwanda	149	275	84.6
Seychelles	19	10	-47.4
Somalia	87	37	-57.5
Tanzania	1,822	1,471	-19.3
Uganda	776	696	-10.3
Zambia	882	859	-2.6
Zimbabwe	2,186	1,999	-8.6
East Africa, Unspecified	1	0	-100.0
Central Africa	**2,371**	**2,331**	**-1.7**
Angola	432	442	2.3
Cameroon	1,171	1,216	3.8
Central African Republic	23	40	73.9
Chad	90	95	5.6
Congo	3	9	200.0
Congo/Zaire	429	340	-20.7
Equatorial Guinea	94	79	-16.0
Gabon	125	105	-16.0
São Tomé & Príncipe	4	5	25.0
North Africa	**5,218**	**4,487**	**-14.0**
Algeria	177	148	-16.4
Egypt	2,155	1,822	-15.5
Libya	33	39	18.2
Morocco	2,034	1,835	-9.8
Sudan	431	279	-35.3
Tunisia	381	341	-10.5
Western Sahara	4	23	475.0
North Africa, Unspecified	3	0	-100.0

Place of Origin	2002/03	2003/04	% Change
Southern Africa	**3,017**	**2,679**	**-11.2**
Botswana	688	488	-29.1
Lesotho	38	39	2.6
Namibia	111	95	-14.4
South Africa	2,095	1,971	-5.9
Swaziland	84	86	2.4
Southern Africa, Unspecified	1	0	-100.0
West Africa	**13,590**	**13,821**	**1.7**
Benin	171	168	-1.8
Burkina Faso	162	191	17.9
Cape Verde	79	52	-34.2
Côte d'Ivoire	675	636	-5.8
Gambia	464	523	12.7
Ghana	3,032	3,288	8.4
Guinea	249	250	0.4
Guinea-Bissau	13	16	23.1
Liberia	531	411	-22.6
Mali	507	378	-25.4
Mauritania	87	68	-21.8
Niger	177	169	-4.5
Nigeria	5,816	6,140	5.6
Senegal	774	805	4.0
Sierra Leone	340	306	-10.0
St. Helena	0	1	-
Togo	498	413	-17.1
West Africa, Unspecified	15	6	-60.0
ASIA	**332,298**	**324,006**	**-2.5**
East Asia	**199,666**	**189,874**	**-4.9**
China	64,757	61,765	-4.6
Hong Kong	8,076	7,353	-9.0
Japan	45,960	40,835	-11.2
Korea, Dem. People's Rep.	213	174	-18.3
Korea, Republic of	51,519	52,484	1.9
Macao	385	374	-2.9
Mongolia	739	711	-3.8
Taiwan	28,017	26,178	-6.6
East Asia, Unspecified	0	0	-
South/Central Asia	**93,767**	**98,138**	**4.7**
Afghanistan	102	109	6.9
Bangladesh	3,596	3,198	-11.1
Bhutan	68	63	-7.4

1   INTERNATIONAL STUDENT TOTALS BY PLACE OF ORIGIN, 2002/03 & 2003/04

Place of Origin	2002/03	2003/04	% Change	Place of Origin	2002/03	2003/04	% Change
India	74,603	79,736	6.9	**Eastern Europe**	**29,167**	**27,710**	**-5.0**
Kazakhstan	556	538	-3.2	Albania	1,106	916	-17.2
Kyrgyzstan	217	179	-17.5	Armenia	390	412	5.6
Nepal	3,729	4,384	17.6	Azerbaijan	277	238	-14.1
Pakistan	8,123	7,325	-9.8	Belarus	417	422	1.2
Republic of Maldives	23	15	-34.8	Bosnia & Herzegovina	528	433	-18.0
Sri Lanka	2,094	1,964	-6.2	Bulgaria	3,725	3,734	0.2
Tajikistan	167	117	-29.9	Croatia	735	660	-10.2
Turkmenistan	102	98	-3.9	Czech Republic	1,180	1,052	-10.8
Uzbekistan	386	412	6.7	Czechoslovakia, Former	0	7	-
S./Central Asia, Unspec.	1	0	-100.0	Estonia	298	271	-9.1
				Georgia	377	373	-1.1
Southeast Asia	**38,865**	**35,994**	**-7.4**	Hungary	1,200	997	-16.9
Brunei	17	13	-23.5	Latvia	447	424	-5.1
Cambodia	329	330	0.3	Lithuania	647	691	6.8
East Timor	4	8	100.0	Macedonia	305	349	14.4
Indonesia	10,432	8,880	-14.9	Moldova	268	266	-0.7
Laos	108	65	-39.8	Poland	2,744	2,913	6.2
Malaysia	6,595	6,483	-1.7	Romania	3,407	3,320	-2.6
Myanmar	870	691	-20.6	Russia	6,238	5,532	-11.3
Philippines	3,576	3,467	-3.0	Slovakia	610	585	-4.1
Singapore	4,189	3,955	-5.6	Slovenia	238	209	-12.2
Thailand	9,982	8,937	-10.5	Ukraine	2,070	2,004	-3.2
Vietnam	2,722	3,165	16.3	U.S.S.R., Former	0	50	-
Southeast Asia, Unspec.	41	0	-100.0	Yugoslavia, Former	1,959	1,851	-5.5
				Eastern Europe, Unspec.	1	1	0.0
MIDDLE EAST	**34,803**	**31,852**	**-8.5**				
Bahrain	451	444	-1.6	**Western Europe**	**48,834**	**46,424**	**-4.9**
Cyprus	1,834	1,562	-14.8	Andorra	11	9	-18.2
Iran	2,258	2,321	2.8	Austria	1,060	899	-15.2
Iraq	127	120	-5.5	Belgium	847	823	-2.8
Israel	3,521	3,474	-1.3	Denmark	901	859	-4.7
Jordan	2,173	1,853	-14.7	Finland	739	619	-16.2
Kuwait	2,212	1,846	-16.5	France	7,223	6,818	-5.6
Lebanon	2,364	2,179	-7.8	Germany	9,302	8,745	-6.0
Oman	540	445	-17.6	Gibraltar	3	0	-100.0
Palestinian Authority	287	247	-13.9	Greece	2,341	2,126	-9.2
Qatar	441	354	-19.7	Iceland	537	488	-9.1
Saudi Arabia	4,175	3,521	-15.7	Ireland	1,055	1,020	-3.3
Syria	642	556	-13.4	Italy	3,287	3,308	0.6
Turkey	11,601	11,398	-1.7	Liechtenstein	9	6	-33.3
United Arab Emirates	1,792	1,248	-30.4	Luxembourg	73	50	-31.5
Yemen	375	284	-24.3	Malta	38	30	-21.1
Middle East, Unspecified	10	0	-100.0	Monaco	13	8	-38.5
				Netherlands	1,672	1,505	-10.0
EUROPE	**78,001**	**74,134**	**-5.0**	Norway	1,568	1,471	-6.2

1   (cont'd) INTERNATIONAL STUDENT TOTALS BY PLACE OF ORIGIN, 2002/03 & 2003/04

Place of Origin	2002/03	2003/04	% Change		Place of Origin	2002/03	2003/04	% Change
Portugal	881	880	-0.1		**South America**	**35,199**	**34,788**	**-1.2**
San Marino	4	2	-50.0		Argentina	3,644	3,644	0.0
Spain	3,633	3,631	-0.1		Bolivia	1,051	1,004	-4.5
Sweden	3,709	3,116	-16.0		Brazil	8,388	7,799	-7.0
Switzerland	1,562	1,561	-0.1		Chile	1,723	1,612	-6.4
United Kingdom	8,326	8,439	1.4		Colombia	7,771	7,533	-3.1
Vatican City	6	11	83.3		Ecuador	2,398	2,345	-2.2
Western Europe, Unspec.	34	0	-100.0		Falkland Islands	0	0	-
					French Guiana	4	1	-75.0
LATIN AMERICA	**68,950**	**69,658**	**1.0**		Guyana	503	503	0.0
					Paraguay	418	343	-17.9
Caribbean	**14,895**	**15,606**	**4.8**		Peru	3,376	3,771	11.7
Anguilla	46	62	34.8		Suriname	97	126	29.9
Antigua	215	240	11.6		Uruguay	493	532	7.9
Aruba	55	60	9.1		Venezuela	5,333	5,575	4.5
Bahamas	2,012	2,030	0.9		South America, Unspec.	0	0	-
Barbados	590	569	-3.6					
British Virgin Islands	113	145	28.3		**NORTH AMERICA**	**27,227**	**27,650**	**1.6**
Cayman Islands	203	191	-5.9		Bermuda	714	633	-11.3
Cuba	141	132	-6.4		Canada	26,513	27,017	1.9
Dominica	288	232	-19.4					
Dominican Republic	983	998	1.5		**OCEANIA**	**4,811**	**4,534**	**-5.8**
Grenada	317	229	-27.8		Australia	2,777	2,706	-2.6
Guadeloupe	8	5	-37.5		Cook Islands	5	3	-40.0
Haiti	910	1,074	18.0		Fed. States of Micronesia	198	182	-8.1
Jamaica	4,723	4,994	5.7		Fiji	212	177	-16.5
Martinique	6	9	50.0		French Polynesia	80	97	21.3
Montserrat	13	6	-53.8		Kiribati	47	53	12.8
Netherlands Antilles	330	225	-31.8		Marshall Islands	31	24	-22.6
St. Kitts-Nevis	172	167	-2.9		Nauru	3	0	-100.0
St. Lucia	331	299	-9.7		New Caledonia	9	9	0.0
St. Vincent	172	183	6.4		New Zealand	1,041	962	-7.6
Trinidad & Tobago	3,127	3,638	16.3		Niue	17	11	-35.3
Turks & Caicos Islands	54	78	44.4		Norfolk Island	1	0	-100.0
Windward Islands	1	0	-100.0		Palau	57	45	-21.1
Caribbean, Unspecified	85	40	-52.9		Papua New Guinea	37	32	-13.5
					Solomon Islands	10	9	-10.0
Central America/Mexico	**18,856**	**19,264**	**2.2**		Tonga	144	111	-22.9
Belize	489	501	2.5		Tuvalu	9	5	-44.4
Costa Rica	951	907	-4.6		Vanuatu	8	5	-37.5
El Salvador	971	976	0.5		Western Samoa	125	103	-17.6
Guatemala	1,045	1,030	-1.4		Pacific Islands, Unspecified	0	0	-
Honduras	985	1,089	10.6					
Mexico	12,801	13,329	4.1		**STATELESS**	**33**	**19**	**-42.4**
Nicaragua	480	473	-1.5					
Panama	1,134	958	-15.5		**UNKNOWN**	**-**	**2,506**	
C. America/Mexico, Unspec.	0	1	-					
					WORLD TOTAL	**586,323**	**572,509**	**-2.4**

1 (cont'd) INTERNATIONAL STUDENT TOTALS BY PLACE OF ORIGIN, 2002/03 & 2003/04

Place of Origin	Under-graduate	% Under-graduate	Graduate	% Graduate	Other	% Other	Total
AFRICA	**25,471**	**66.8**	**11,308**	**29.6**	**1,371**	**3.6**	**38,150**
Africa, Unspecified	1	100.0	0	0.0	0	0.0	1
East Africa	**10,778**	**72.7**	**3,684**	**24.8**	**369**	**2.5**	**14,831**
Burundi	71	88.8	7	8.8	2	2.5	80
Comoros	20	90.9	2	9.1	0	0.0	22
Djibouti	2	100.0	0	0.0	0	0.0	2
Eritrea	36	28.3	85	66.9	6	4.7	127
Ethiopia	650	61.3	380	35.8	30	2.8	1,060
Kenya	5,297	71.8	1,873	25.4	211	2.9	7,381
Madagascar	39	35.8	68	62.4	2	1.8	109
Malawi	273	68.4	123	30.8	3	0.8	399
Mauritius	147	70.3	56	26.8	6	2.9	209
Mozambique	44	47.3	46	49.5	3	3.2	93
Reunion	2	100.0	0	0.0	0	0.0	2
Rwanda	209	76.0	57	20.7	9	3.3	275
Seychelles	9	90.0	1	10.0	0	0.0	10
Somalia	30	81.1	7	18.9	0	0.0	37
Tanzania	1,093	74.3	341	23.2	37	2.5	1,471
Uganda	382	54.9	293	42.1	21	3.0	696
Zambia	674	78.5	165	19.2	20	2.3	859
Zimbabwe	1,800	90.0	180	9.0	19	1.0	1,999
Central Africa	**1,694**	**72.7**	**534**	**22.9**	**103**	**4.4**	**2,331**
Angola	341	77.1	86	19.5	15	3.4	442
Cameroon	848	69.7	326	26.8	42	3.5	1,216
Central African Republic	32	80.0	6	15.0	2	5.0	40
Chad	72	75.8	12	12.6	11	11.6	95
Congo	3	33.3	6	66.7	0	0.0	9
Congo/Zaire	251	73.8	70	20.6	19	5.6	340
Equatorial Guinea	65	82.3	6	7.6	8	10.1	79
Gabon	78	74.3	21	20.0	6	5.7	105
São Tomé & Príncipe	4	80.0	1	20.0	0	0.0	5
North Africa	**2,096**	**46.7**	**2,139**	**47.7**	**252**	**5.6**	**4,487**
Algeria	63	42.6	77	52.0	8	5.4	148
Egypt	490	26.9	1,242	68.2	90	4.9	1,822
Libya	27	69.2	8	20.5	4	10.3	39
Morocco	1,174	64.0	550	30.0	111	6.0	1,835
Sudan	152	54.5	119	42.7	8	2.9	279
Tunisia	170	49.9	140	41.1	31	9.1	341
Western Sahara	20	87.0	3	13.0	0	0.0	23
North Africa, Unspecified	0	0.0	0	0.0	0	0.0	0
Southern Africa	**1,612**	**60.2**	**949**	**35.4**	**118**	**4.4**	**2,679**

2   INTERNATIONAL STUDENTS BY ACADEMIC LEVEL AND PLACE OF ORIGIN, 2003/04

Place of Origin	Under-graduate	% Under-graduate	Graduate	% Graduate	Other	% Other	Total
Botswana	270	55.3	194	39.8	24	4.9	488
Lesotho	25	64.1	14	35.9	0	0.0	39
Namibia	59	62.1	32	33.7	4	4.2	95
South Africa	1,193	60.5	690	35.0	88	4.5	1,971
Swaziland	65	75.6	19	22.1	2	2.3	86
West Africa	**9,290**	**67.2**	**4,002**	**29.0**	**529**	**3.8**	**13,821**
Benin	95	56.5	65	38.7	8	4.8	168
Burkina Faso	133	69.6	52	27.2	6	3.1	191
Cape Verde	38	73.1	9	17.3	5	9.6	52
Côte d'Ivoire	394	61.9	177	27.8	65	10.2	636
Gambia	466	89.1	51	9.8	6	1.1	523
Ghana	1,828	55.6	1,338	40.7	122	3.7	3,288
Guinea	192	76.8	30	12.0	28	11.2	250
Guinea-Bissau	13	81.3	3	18.8	0	0.0	16
Liberia	310	75.4	95	23.1	6	1.5	411
Mali	278	73.5	64	16.9	36	9.5	378
Mauritania	47	69.1	13	19.1	8	11.8	68
Niger	113	66.9	49	29.0	7	4.1	169
Nigeria	4,287	69.8	1,680	27.4	173	2.8	6,140
Senegal	573	71.2	200	24.8	32	4.0	805
Sierra Leone	187	61.1	113	36.9	6	2.0	306
St. Helena	1	100.0	0	0.0	0	0.0	1
Togo	332	80.4	60	14.5	21	5.1	413
West Africa, Unspecified	3	50.0	3	50.0	0	0.0	6
ASIA	**118,522**	**36.6**	**184,300**	**56.9**	**21,184**	**6.5**	**324,006**
East Asia	**73,546**	**38.7**	**101,028**	**53.2**	**15,300**	**8.1**	**189,874**
China	8,034	13.0	50,796	82.2	2,935	4.8	61,765
Hong Kong	5,494	74.7	1,465	19.9	394	5.4	7,353
Japan	27,925	68.4	8,681	21.3	4,229	10.4	40,835
Korea, Dem. People's Rep.	134	77.0	34	19.5	6	3.4	174
Korea, Republic of	22,727	43.3	24,757	47.2	5,000	9.5	52,484
Macao	297	79.4	70	18.7	7	1.9	374
Mongolia	434	61.0	210	29.5	67	9.4	711
Taiwan	8,501	32.5	15,015	57.4	2,662	10.2	26,178
South/Central Asia	**24,611**	**25.1**	**69,624**	**70.9**	**3,903**	**4.0**	**98,138**
Afghanistan	81	74.3	19	17.4	9	8.3	109
Bangladesh	1,563	48.9	1,512	47.3	123	3.8	3,198
Bhutan	36	57.1	26	41.3	1	1.6	63
India	13,531	17.0	63,013	79.0	3,192	4.0	79,736
Kazakhstan	267	49.6	237	44.1	34	6.3	538

2   (cont'd) INTERNATIONAL STUDENTS BY ACADEMIC LEVEL AND PLACE OF ORIGIN, 2003/04

Place of Origin	Under-graduate	% Under-graduate	Graduate	% Graduate	Other	% Other	Total
Kyrgyzstan	94	52.5	77	43.0	8	4.5	179
Nepal	3,017	68.8	1,208	27.6	159	3.6	4,384
Pakistan	4,636	63.3	2,408	32.9	281	3.8	7,325
Republic of Maldives	10	66.7	5	33.3	0	0.0	15
Sri Lanka	1,015	51.7	883	45.0	66	3.4	1,964
Tajikistan	85	72.6	25	21.4	7	6.0	117
Turkmenistan	59	60.2	39	39.8	0	0.0	98
Uzbekistan	217	52.7	172	41.7	23	5.6	412
Southeast Asia	**20,365**	**56.6**	**13,648**	**37.9**	**1,981**	**5.5**	**35,994**
Brunei	7	53.8	5	38.5	1	7.7	13
Cambodia	240	72.7	62	18.8	28	8.5	330
East Timor	6	75.0	2	25.0	0	0.0	8
Indonesia	6,249	70.4	2,190	24.7	441	5.0	8,880
Laos	48	73.8	10	15.4	7	10.8	65
Malaysia	4,543	70.1	1,731	26.7	209	3.2	6,483
Myanmar	501	72.5	167	24.2	23	3.3	691
Philippines	1,911	55.1	1,368	39.5	188	5.4	3,467
Singapore	2,170	54.9	1,590	40.2	195	4.9	3,955
Thailand	2,464	27.6	5,708	63.9	765	8.6	8,937
Vietnam	2,226	70.3	815	25.8	124	3.9	3,165
MIDDLE EAST	**14,543**	**45.7**	**15,358**	**48.2**	**1,951**	**6.1**	**31,852**
Bahrain	348	78.4	90	20.3	6	1.4	444
Cyprus	876	56.1	622	39.8	64	4.1	1,562
Iran	785	33.8	1,429	61.6	107	4.6	2,321
Iraq	74	61.7	40	33.3	6	5.0	120
Israel	1,530	44.0	1,711	49.3	233	6.7	3,474
Jordan	671	36.2	1,100	59.4	82	4.4	1,853
Kuwait	1,350	73.1	383	20.7	113	6.1	1,846
Lebanon	1,070	49.1	984	45.2	125	5.7	2,179
Oman	317	71.2	115	25.8	13	2.9	445
Palestinian Authority	111	44.9	111	44.9	25	10.1	247
Qatar	292	82.5	44	12.4	18	5.1	354
Saudi Arabia	2,022	57.4	1,290	36.6	209	5.9	3,521
Syria	267	48.0	248	44.6	41	7.4	556
Turkey	3,665	32.2	6,912	60.6	821	7.2	11,398
United Arab Emirates	990	79.3	191	15.3	67	5.4	1,248
Yemen	175	61.6	88	31.0	21	7.4	284
EUROPE	**35,527**	**47.9**	**32,845**	**44.3**	**5,762**	**7.8**	**74,134**
Eastern Europe	**13,543**	**48.9**	**12,905**	**46.6**	**1,262**	**4.6**	**27,710**
Albania	632	69.0	233	25.4	51	5.6	916

2 (cont'd) INTERNATIONAL STUDENTS BY ACADEMIC LEVEL AND PLACE OF ORIGIN, 2003/04

Place of Origin	Under-graduate	% Under-graduate	Graduate	% Graduate	Other	% Other	Total
Armenia	112	27.2	269	65.3	31	7.5	412
Azerbaijan	83	34.9	142	59.7	13	5.5	238
Belarus	219	51.9	189	44.8	14	3.3	422
Bosnia & Herzegovina	296	68.4	121	27.9	16	3.7	433
Bulgaria	2,274	60.9	1,299	34.8	161	4.3	3,734
Croatia	342	51.8	293	44.4	25	3.8	660
Czech Republic	628	59.7	368	35.0	56	5.3	1,052
Czechoslovakia, Former	4	57.1	3	42.9	0	0.0	7
Estonia	171	63.1	83	30.6	17	6.3	271
Georgia	151	40.5	201	53.9	21	5.6	373
Hungary	116	11.6	869	87.2	12	1.2	997
Latvia	288	67.9	121	28.5	15	3.5	424
Lithuania	475	68.7	196	28.4	20	2.9	691
Macedonia	208	59.6	123	35.2	18	5.2	349
Moldova	146	54.9	108	40.6	12	4.5	266
Poland	1,895	65.1	862	29.6	156	5.4	2,913
Romania	922	27.8	2,290	69.0	108	3.3	3,320
Russia	2,322	42.0	2,865	51.8	345	6.2	5,532
Slovakia	328	56.1	233	39.8	24	4.1	585
Slovenia	99	47.4	103	49.3	7	3.3	209
Ukraine	758	37.8	1,170	58.4	76	3.8	2,004
U.S.S.R., Former	34	68.0	15	30.0	1	2.0	50
Yugoslavia, Former	1,039	56.1	749	40.5	63	3.4	1,851
Eastern Europe, Unspecified	1	100.0	0	0.0	0	0.0	1
Western Europe	**21,984**	**47.4**	**19,940**	**43.0**	**4,500**	**9.7**	**46,424**
Andorra	6	66.7	3	33.3	0	0.0	9
Austria	456	50.7	349	38.8	94	10.5	899
Belgium	351	42.6	401	48.7	71	8.6	823
Denmark	403	46.9	348	40.5	108	12.6	859
Finland	354	57.2	221	35.7	44	7.1	619
France	2,755	40.4	3,196	46.9	867	12.7	6,818
Germany	3,926	44.9	3,915	44.8	904	10.3	8,745
Greece	580	27.3	1,434	67.5	112	5.3	2,126
Iceland	222	45.5	248	50.8	18	3.7	488
Ireland	507	49.7	426	41.8	87	8.5	1,020
Italy	994	30.0	1,995	60.3	319	9.6	3,308
Liechtenstein	0	0.0	4	66.7	2	33.3	6
Luxembourg	32	64.0	16	32.0	2	4.0	50
Malta	9	30.0	20	66.7	1	3.3	30
Monaco	4	50.0	4	50.0	0	0.0	8
Netherlands	802	53.3	539	35.8	164	10.9	1,505
Norway	874	59.4	420	28.6	177	12.0	1,471
Portugal	365	41.5	474	53.9	41	4.7	880

2 (cont'd) INTERNATIONAL STUDENTS BY ACADEMIC LEVEL AND PLACE OF ORIGIN, 2003/04

Place of Origin	Under-graduate	% Under-graduate	Graduate	% Graduate	Other	% Other	Total
San Marino	1	50.0	1	50.0	0	0.0	2
Spain	1,388	38.2	1,879	51.7	364	10.0	3,631
Sweden	2,253	72.3	606	19.4	257	8.2	3,116
Switzerland	734	47.0	665	42.6	162	10.4	1,561
United Kingdom	4,962	58.8	2,775	32.9	702	8.3	8,439
Vatican City	6	54.5	1	9.1	4	36.4	11
LATIN AMERICA	**44,584**	**64.0**	**21,460**	**30.8**	**3,614**	**5.2**	**69,658**
Caribbean	**12,182**	**78.1**	**3,095**	**19.8**	**329**	**2.1**	**15,606**
Anguilla	40	64.5	22	35.5	0	0.0	62
Antigua	190	79.2	46	19.2	4	1.7	240
Aruba	52	86.7	8	13.3	0	0.0	60
Bahamas	1,647	81.1	340	16.7	43	2.1	2,030
Barbados	358	62.9	184	32.3	27	4.7	569
British Virgin Islands	122	84.1	21	14.5	2	1.4	145
Cayman Islands	169	88.5	20	10.5	2	1.0	191
Cuba	99	75.0	27	20.5	6	4.5	132
Dominica	184	79.3	45	19.4	3	1.3	232
Dominican Republic	720	72.1	233	23.3	45	4.5	998
Grenada	160	69.9	61	26.6	8	3.5	229
Guadeloupe	5	100.0	0	0.0	0	0.0	5
Haiti	928	86.4	127	11.8	19	1.8	1,074
Jamaica	3,775	75.6	1,122	22.5	97	1.9	4,994
Martinique	8	88.9	1	11.1	0	0.0	9
Montserrat	4	66.7	2	33.3	0	0.0	6
Netherlands Antilles	182	80.9	30	13.3	13	5.8	225
St. Kitts-Nevis	119	71.3	47	28.1	1	0.6	167
St. Lucia	230	76.9	68	22.7	1	0.3	299
St. Vincent	155	84.7	28	15.3	0	0.0	183
Trinidad & Tobago	2,940	80.8	640	17.6	58	1.6	3,638
Turks & Caicos Islands	63	80.8	15	19.2	0	0.0	78
Caribbean, Unspecified	32	80.0	8	20.0	0	0.0	40
Central America/Mexico	**12,574**	**65.3**	**5,699**	**29.6**	**991**	**5.1**	**19,264**
Belize	365	72.9	130	25.9	6	1.2	501
Costa Rica	456	50.3	407	44.9	44	4.9	907
El Salvador	768	78.7	163	16.7	45	4.6	976
Guatemala	766	74.4	238	23.1	26	2.5	1,030
Honduras	861	79.1	201	18.5	27	2.5	1,089
Mexico	8,303	62.3	4,225	31.7	801	6.0	13,329
Nicaragua	360	76.1	102	21.6	11	2.3	473
Panama	695	72.5	232	24.2	31	3.2	958
C. America/Mexico, Unspec.	0	0.0	1	100.0	0	0.0	1

2 (cont'd) INTERNATIONAL STUDENTS BY ACADEMIC LEVEL AND PLACE OF ORIGIN, 2003/04

Place of Origin	Under-graduate	% Under-graduate	Graduate	% Graduate	Other	% Other	Total
South America	**19,828**	**57.0**	**12,666**	**36.4**	**2,294**	**6.6**	**34,788**
Argentina	1,504	41.3	1,927	52.9	213	5.8	3,644
Bolivia	853	85.0	124	12.4	27	2.7	1,004
Brazil	4,243	54.4	3,018	38.7	538	6.9	7,799
Chile	589	36.5	889	55.1	134	8.3	1,612
Colombia	4,342	57.6	2,686	35.7	505	6.7	7,533
Ecuador	1,631	69.6	582	24.8	132	5.6	2,345
French Guiana	0	0.0	1	100.0	0	0.0	1
Guyana	393	78.1	103	20.5	7	1.4	503
Paraguay	233	67.9	87	25.4	23	6.7	343
Peru	2,206	58.5	1,349	35.8	216	5.7	3,771
Suriname	81	64.3	44	34.9	1	0.8	126
Uruguay	216	40.6	279	52.4	37	7.0	532
Venezuela	3,537	63.4	1,577	28.3	461	8.3	5,575
NORTH AMERICA	**14,506**	**52.5**	**12,237**	**44.3**	**907**	**3.3**	**27,650**
Bermuda	510	80.6	108	17.1	15	2.4	633
Canada	13,996	51.8	12,129	44.9	892	3.3	27,017
OCEANIA	**2,696**	**59.5**	**1,559**	**34.4**	**279**	**6.2**	**4,534**
Australia	1,474	54.5	1,020	37.7	212	7.8	2,706
Cook Islands	2	66.7	1	33.3	0	0.0	3
Fed. States of Micronesia	176	96.7	6	3.3	0	0.0	182
Fiji	159	89.8	17	9.6	1	0.6	177
French Polynesia	83	85.6	5	5.2	9	9.3	97
Kiribati	44	83.0	7	13.2	2	3.8	53
Marshall Islands	24	100.0	0	0.0	0	0.0	24
New Caledonia	8	88.9	0	0.0	1	11.1	9
New Zealand	446	46.4	464	48.2	52	5.4	962
Niue	7	63.6	4	36.4	0	0.0	11
Palau	45	100.0	0	0.0	0	0.0	45
Papua New Guinea	22	68.8	10	31.3	0	0.0	32
Solomon Islands	5	55.6	4	44.4	0	0.0	9
Tonga	104	93.7	6	5.4	1	0.9	111
Tuvalu	3	60.0	2	40.0	0	0.0	5
Vanuatu	4	80.0	1	20.0	0	0.0	5
Western Samoa	90	87.4	12	11.7	1	1.0	103
STATELESS	**10**	**52.6**	**9**	**47.4**	**0**	**0.0**	**19**
UNKNOWN	-	-	-	-	-	-	**2,506**
WORLD TOTAL*	**255,859**	**44.7**	**279,076**	**48.7**	**35,068**	**6.1**	**572,509**

* Academic level totals by place of origin differ from the "official" academic level totals reported in Table 18 and throughout, due to the difference in responses from some of the institutions to the nationality and academic level survey questions.

2 (cont'd) INTERNATIONAL STUDENTS BY ACADEMIC LEVEL AND PLACE OF ORIGIN, 2003/04

Rank	Metropolitan/Micropolitan Statistical Area * **	Int'l Students
1	New York-Newark-Edison, NY-NJ-PA	52,424
2	Los Angeles-Long Beach-Santa Ana, CA	35,062
3	Boston-Cambridge-Quincy, MA-NH	24,266
4	Washington-Arlington-Alexandria, DC-VA-MD-WV	19,552
5	Chicago-Naperville-Joliet, IL-IN-WI	16,061
6	San Francisco-Oakland-Fremont, CA	13,460
7	Dallas-Fort Worth-Arlington, TX	13,448
8	Philadelphia-Camden-Wilmington, PA-NJ-DE-MD	12,593
9	Miami-Fort Lauderdale-Miami Beach, FL	11,900
10	Houston-Baytown-Sugar Land, TX	9,778
Total of Top 10		**208,544**
11	San Jose-Sunnyvale-Santa Clara, CA	9,512
12	Atlanta-Sandy Springs-Marietta, GA	8,191
13	Seattle-Tacoma-Bellevue, WA	7,838
14	Austin-Round Rock, TX	6,561
15	San Diego-Carlsbad-San Marcos, CA	6,249
16	Detroit-Warren-Livonia, MI	6,088
17	Buffalo-Cheektowaga-Tonawanda, NY	6,026
18	Phoenix-Mesa-Scottsdale, AZ	5,956
19	Ann Arbor, MI	5,685
20	Minneapolis-St. Paul-Bloomington, MN-WI	5,683
21	Pittsburgh, PA	5,680
22	Baltimore-Towson, MD	5,620
23	Columbus, OH	5,557
24	Champaign-Urbana, IL	5,112
25	Lafayette, IN	5,110
26	Honolulu, HI	5,009
27	Oklahoma City, OK	4,727
28	St. Louis, MO-IL	4,614
29	State College, PA	4,101
30	College Station-Bryan, TX	3,815
30	Lansing-East Lansing, MI	3,815
32	Providence-New Bedford-Fall River, RI-MA	3,780
33	Bloomington, IN	3,715
34	Madison, WI	3,553
35	Gainesville, FL	3,546
36	Tucson, AZ	3,450
37	Tampa-St. Petersburg-Clearwater, FL	3,352
38	Riverside-San Bernardino-Ontario, CA	3,157
39	Durham, NC	3,143
40	Hartford-West Hartford-East Hartford, CT	3,099
41	Ithaca, NY	3,027
42	Sacramento—Arden-Arcade—Roseville, CA	3,025
43	Rochester, NY	2,983

3 ENROLLMENTS IN METROPOLITAN AND MICROPOLITAN STATISTICAL AREAS WITH MORE THAN 1,000 INTERNATIONAL STUDENTS, 2003/04

Rank	Metropolitan/Micropolitan Statistical Area * **	Int'l Students
44	Cincinnati-Middletown, OH-KY-IN	2,978
45	Cleveland-Elyria-Mentor, OH	2,923
46	Denver-Aurora, CO	2,846
47	Syracuse, NY	2,744
48	El Paso, TX	2,702
49	New Haven-Milford, CT	2,612
50	Springfield, MA	2,605
51	Provo-Orem, UT	2,556
52	Orlando, FL	2,504
53	Portland-Vancouver-Beaverton, OR-WA	2,372
54	New Orleans-Metairie-Kenner, LA	2,329
55	Iowa City, IA	2,306
56	Ames, IA	2,302
57	Blacksburg-Christiansburg-Radford, VA	2,281
58	Albany-Schenectady-Troy, NY	2,206
59	Stillwater, OK Micropolitan Statistical Area	2,168
60	Salt Lake City, UT	2,137
61	Kansas City, MO-KS	2,094
62	Virginia Beach-Norfolk-Newport News, VA-NC	1,959
63	Baton Rouge, LA	1,944
64	Raleigh-Cary, NC	1,886
65	Kalamazoo-Portage, MI	1,885
66	Wichita, KS	1,822
67	Las Vegas-Paradise, NV	1,808
68	Eugene-Springfield, OR	1,807
69	Toledo, OH	1,776
70	Bridgeport-Stamford-Norwalk, CT	1,750
71	Akron, OH	1,736
72	Milwaukee-Waukesha-West Allis, WI	1,722
73	San Antonio, TX	1,707
74	Carbondale, IL Micropolitan Statistical Area	1,704
75	Lawrence, KS	1,647
76	Lexington-Fayette, KY	1,602
77	Santa Barbara-Santa Maria-Goleta, CA	1,592
78	Memphis, TN-MS-AR	1,589
79	Lincoln, NE	1,565
80	Trenton-Ewing, NJ	1,550
81	Nashville-Davidson—Murfreesboro, TN	1,519
82	Columbia, MO	1,513
83	Columbia, SC	1,469
84	Athens, OH Micropolitan Statistical Area	1,452
84	Charlottesville, VA	1,452
86	Worcester, MA	1,445
87	Indianapolis, IN	1,429
88	Omaha-Council Bluffs, NE-IA	1,427
89	Athens-Clarke County, GA	1,408

3 (cont'd) ENROLLMENTS IN METROPOLITAN AND MICROPOLITAN STATISTICAL AREAS WITH MORE THAN 1,000 INTERNATIONAL STUDENTS, 2003/04

Rank	Metropolitan/Micropolitan Statistical Area * **	Int'l Students
90	Morgantown, WV	1,403
91	Tallahassee, FL	1,398
92	Binghamton, NY	1,326
93	South Bend-Mishawaka, IN-MI	1,321
94	Birmingham-Hoover, AL	1,304
95	Boulder, CO	1,273
96	Pullman, WA Micropolitan Statistical Area	1,250
97	Dayton, OH	1,222
98	Fayetteville-Springdale-Rogers, AR-MO	1,219
99	Lubbock, TX	1,195
100	Tulsa, OK	1,193
101	Charlotte-Gastonia-Concord, NC-SC	1,165
102	Knoxville, TN	1,128
103	Louisville, KY-IN	1,117
104	St. Cloud, MN	1,097
105	Fresno, CA	1,087
106	Corvallis, OR	1,063
107	Mobile, AL	1,052
108	Richmond, VA	1,021
109	Greenville, SC	1,005

* Due to some of the changes in county compositions for many Metropolitan Statistical Areas in 2003, as well as the creation of Micropolitan Statistical Areas, comparisons with prior years' *Open Doors* is not feasible.

** Metropolitan Statistical Area, unless otherwise noted as Micropolitan Statistical Area

3 (cont'd) ENROLLMENTS IN METROPOLITAN AND MICROPOLITAN STATISTICAL AREAS WITH MORE THAN 1,000 INTERNATIONAL STUDENTS, 2003/04

State/Region	1959/60	1969/70	1979/80	1989/90	1999/00	2000/01	2001/02	2002/03	2003/04	% Change from 2002/03
Alaska	0	73	185	364	392	518	479	393	427	8.7
California	6,457	22,170	47,621	54,178	66,305	74,281	78,741	80,487	77,186	-4.1
Hawaii	151	1,927	2,653	4,190	5,430	5,344	5,289	5,437	5,371	-1.2
Oregon	638	2,312	4,853	6,403	6,404	6,612	6,560	6,436	5,855	-9.0
Washington	1,031	3,238	6,717	6,858	10,965	11,370	11,624	11,430	10,756	-5.9
Pacific Totals	**8,277**	**29,720**	**62,029**	**71,993**	**89,496**	**98,125**	**102,693**	**104,183**	**99,595**	**-4.4**
Colorado	672	1,460	4,184	4,681	6,461	6,442	6,692	6,295	5,943	-5.6
Idaho	160	500	989	1,150	1,271	1,448	1,578	1,727	1,727	0.0
Montana	162	324	401	770	1,011	998	944	871	872	0.1
Nevada	12	109	521	783	2,450	2,755	2,927	2,702	2,743	1.5
Utah	741	1,915	3,493	4,862	5,834	6,077	5,950	6,022	5,781	-4.0
Wyoming	63	282	435	527	487	446	448	491	493	0.4
Mountain Totals	**1,810**	**4,590**	**10,023**	**12,773**	**17,514**	**18,166**	**18,539**	**18,108**	**17,559**	**-3.0**
Illinois	2,890	7,795	12,218	16,816	22,807	24,229	25,498	27,116	25,609	-5.6
Indiana	1,819	3,230	5,499	7,575	11,654	12,019	12,871	13,529	13,586	0.4
Iowa	776	1,285	4,010	6,735	7,218	7,840	7,896	7,815	7,699	-1.5
Kansas	800	2,005	4,479	6,009	6,050	6,533	7,240	7,000	6,573	-6.1
Michigan	3,259	6,774	10,559	13,555	19,151	21,120	23,103	22,873	22,277	-2.6
Minnesota	1,473	2,577	4,142	5,446	7,888	8,473	8,651	8,985	9,142	1.7
Missouri	996	2,896	4,712	6,620	9,182	10,042	10,281	10,181	9,973	-2.0
Nebraska	358	601	1,517	1,918	3,317	3,223	3,874	3,689	3,524	-4.5
North Dakota	211	616	512	1,341	991	1,126	1,376	1,485	1,595	7.4
Ohio	1,550	4,121	8,672	13,856	16,806	18,502	19,384	18,668	18,770	0.5
South Dakota	113	262	486	758	700	745	770	774	739	-4.5
Wisconsin	1,199	3,450	4,088	6,438	7,833	7,749	7,701	8,058	7,142	-11.4
Midwest Totals	**15,444**	**35,612**	**60,894**	**87,067**	**113,597**	**121,601**	**128,645**	**130,173**	**126,629**	**-2.7**
Alabama	311	551	3,220	4,513	5,441	5,600	6,040	6,384	6,386	0.0
Arkansas	107	235	1,328	1,710	2,317	2,649	2,758	2,679	2,781	3.8
Delaware	38	311	447	1,003	2,016	2,091	1,975	2,230	2,142	-3.9
District of Columbia	2,020	3,949	8,499	9,487	8,202	9,094	9,241	8,892	8,532	-4.0
Florida	730	6,939	11,919	20,364	24,827	25,366	28,303	27,270	25,861	-5.2
Georgia	416	1,258	4,472	5,980	9,901	10,844	11,991	12,267	12,010	-2.1
Kentucky	293	734	2,208	2,543	4,201	4,778	4,789	5,018	4,751	-5.3
Louisiana	815	1,720	5,546	5,535	6,305	6,400	6,312	6,533	6,621	1.3
Maryland	542	1,670	4,266	6,952	11,941	12,409	13,947	12,749	12,633	-0.9
Mississippi	130	387	1,704	1,941	2,263	2,331	2,381	2,143	2,280	6.4
North Carolina	628	1,594	3,709	5,764	7,848	7,957	8,960	8,599	8,826	2.6
South Carolina	185	368	1,484	2,381	3,523	3,573	3,731	3,977	3,919	-1.5
Tennessee	450	1,295	4,499	4,247	5,244	5,835	5,867	5,687	5,846	2.8
Virginia	275	662	3,374	6,970	11,616	12,782	12,600	12,875	12,531	-2.7
West Virginia	118	226	1,453	1,417	2,230	2,032	2,108	2,173	2,507	15.4
South Totals	**7,058**	**21,899**	**58,128**	**80,807**	**107,875**	**113,741**	**121,003**	**119,476**	**117,626**	**-1.5**

4   INTERNATIONAL STUDENTS IN U.S. STATES AND REGIONS, SELECTED YEARS 1959/60 – 2003/04

State/Region	1959/60	1969/70	1979/80	1989/90	1999/00	2000/01	2001/02	2002/03	2003/04	% Change from 2002/03
Arizona	310	1,134	3,798	6,763	9,405	9,912	10,511	10,325	9,907	-4.0
New Mexico	515	481	1,240	1,399	1,672	1,629	1,893	1,978	2,111	6.7
Oklahoma	717	1,554	8,464	5,989	8,041	8,263	8,818	9,026	8,764	-2.9
Texas	1,574	4,902	24,416	24,170	35,860	37,735	44,192	45,672	45,150	-1.1
Southwest Totals	**3,116**	**8,071**	**37,918**	**38,321**	**54,978**	**57,539**	**65,414**	**67,001**	**65,932**	**-1.6**
Connecticut	573	1,314	2,847	4,636	7,110	7,358	8,050	6,603	7,655	15.9
Maine	84	262	307	902	1,282	1,256	1,357	1,383	1,730	25.1
Massachusetts	3,136	6,352	12,607	20,840	28,192	29,395	29,988	30,039	28,634	-4.7
New Hampshire	102	356	501	1,262	2,068	2,301	2,436	2,359	2,128	-9.8
New Jersey	583	1,738	4,767	9,608	12,179	12,558	13,516	13,644	13,163	-3.5
New York	6,069	17,701	23,509	38,350	55,085	58,286	62,053	63,773	63,313	-0.7
Pennsylvania	1,734	5,248	8,919	15,803	20,336	22,279	24,014	24,470	23,428	-4.3
Rhode Island	191	635	949	1,858	3,176	3,375	3,370	3,193	3,337	4.5
Vermont	136	222	702	1,206	959	949	908	903	835	-7.5
Northeast Totals	**12,608**	**33,828**	**55,108**	**94,465**	**130,387**	**137,757**	**145,692**	**146,367**	**144,223**	**-1.5**
Guam	-	113	589	473	106	161	162	161	69	-57.1
Puerto Rico	156	1,049	628	633	621	672	743	853	876	2.7
Virgin Islands	-	104	130	319	149	105	105	0*	0*	-
Other Totals	**156**	**1,266**	**1,347**	**1,425**	**876**	**938**	**1,010**	**1,014**	**945**	**-6.8**
U.S. TOTAL	**48,486**	**134,959**	**286,343**	**386,851**	**514,723**	**547,867**	**582,996**	**586,323**	**572,509**	**-2.4**

* Did not report

4   (cont'd) INTERNATIONAL STUDENTS IN U.S. STATES AND REGIONS, SELECTED YEARS 1959/60 – 2003/04

Primary Source of Funds	2002/03 Int'l Students	2002/03 % of Total	2003/04 Int'l Students	2003/04 % of Total	% Change
Personal & Family	385,889	65.8	385,543	67.3	-0.1
U.S. College or University	124,298	21.2	134,015	23.4	7.8
Home Government/University	16,273	2.8	13,699	2.4	-15.8
U.S. Private Sponsor	14,366	2.5	2,921	0.5	-79.7
Foreign Private Sponsor	19,561	3.3	12,326	2.2	-37.0
Current Employment	11,119	1.9	11,888	2.1	6.9
U.S. Government	3,085	0.5	10,111	1.8	227.7
International Organization	1,693	0.3	1,964	0.3	16.0
Other Sources	10,038	1.7	42	0.0	-99.6
Total	**586,323**	**100.0**	**572,509**	**100.0**	**-2.4**

5   INTERNATIONAL STUDENTS BY PRIMARY SOURCE OF FUNDS, 2002/03 & 2003/04

Primary Source of Funds	% Under- graduate	% Graduate	% Other
Personal & Family	81.8	51.6	69.7
U.S. College or University	10.1	40.4	7.8
Home Government/University	2.0	2.2	4.1
U.S. Government	0.3	0.7	0.3
U.S. Private Sponsor	2.8	1.5	2.0
Foreign Private Sponsor	2.6	1.7	1.3
Current Employment	0.3	0.4	13.9
International Organization	0.2	1.4	0.8
Other Sources	0.0	0.0	0.0
Total	**100.0**	**100.0**	**100.0**

6   PRIMARY SOURCE OF FUNDING WITHIN ACADEMIC LEVEL, 2003/04

Carnegie Category*	1999/00	2000/01	2001/02	2002/03	2003/04	% Change from 2002/03	% Changes 1999-2004
TOTAL CENSUS	**514,723**	**547,867**	**582,996**	**586,323**	**572,509**	**-2.4**	**11.2**
Doctoral/Research Extensive	258,116	273,974	291,137	296,269	293,072	-1.1	13.5
Doctoral/Research Intensive	54,861	57,478	62,301	62,672	61,767	-1.4	12.6
All Doctoral/Research	**312,977**	**331,452**	**353,438**	**358,941**	**354,839**	**-1.1**	**13.4**
Master's I	80,015	86,299	91,749	90,999	88,791	-2.4	11.0
Master's II	4,739	5,523	5,380	4,621	4,896	6.0	3.3
All Master's	**84,754**	**91,822**	**97,129**	**95,620**	**93,687**	**-2.0**	**10.5**
Baccalaureate – Liberal Arts	10,245	9,864	11,046	11,028	11,139	1.0	8.7
Baccalaureate – General	10,122	10,186	10,719	11,370	11,555	1.6	14.2
Baccalaureate/Associate's	2,525	2,770	2,671	2,749	2,682	-2.4	6.2
All Baccalaureate	**22,892**	**22,820**	**24,436**	**25,147**	**25,376**	**0.9**	**10.9**
Associate's	**70,616**	**76,834**	**82,932**	**82,123**	**75,830**	**-7.7**	**7.4**
Religious	2,875	2,856	2,888	3,081	3,027	-1.8	5.3
Medical	1,714	1,781	1,934	2,182	2,271	4.1	32.5
Other Health	2,456	3,088	3,385	2,331	2,377	2.0	-3.2
Engineering	1,962	2,188	2,353	2,292	2,093	-8.7	6.7
Business	4,823	5,103	4,964	4,923	3,755	-23.7	-22.1
Fine Arts	8,417	8,602	8,308	8,318	7,973	-4.1	-5.3
Law	243	278	243	240	239	-0.4	-1.6
Teachers'	114	113	94	95	51	-46.3	-55.3
Other Specialized	880	928	890	1,029	990	-3.8	12.5
Tribal Colleges	0	2	2	1	1	0.0	-
All Specialized	**23,484**	**24,939**	**25,061**	**24,492**	**22,777**	**-7.0**	**-3.0**

* Based on the 2000 Carnegie Classification of Institutions of Higher Education codes. These are not entirely comparable to the codes used in previous *Open Doors*, which were based upon the 1994 Carnegie classifications. For more information, see *http://www.carnegiefoundation.org/classification/index.htm*.

7   INTERNATIONAL STUDENT ENROLLMENTS BY INSTITUTIONAL TYPE, 1999/00 – 2003/04

8 TOP 20 PLACES OF ORIGIN OF INTERNATIONAL STUDENTS BY INSTITUTIONAL TYPE, 2003/04

RANK	DOCTORAL/RESEARCH EXTENSIVE & INTENSIVE		MASTER'S I&II		BACCALAUREATE I&II, BACCALAUREATE/ASSOCIATE'S		ASSOCIATE'S		OTHER INSTITUTIONS	
	Place of Origin	% of Enrollment	Place of Origin	% of Enrollment	Place of Origin	% of Enrollment	Place of Origin	% of Enrollment	Place of Origin	% of Enrollment
1	India	17.5	India	12.3	Japan	10.2	Japan	15.3	Korea, Rep. of	17.6
2	China	14.5	Japan	10.1	Canada	10.1	Korea, Rep. of	9.1	Canada	13.0
3	Korea, Rep. of	9.7	Taiwan	6.0	Korea, Rep. of	6.4	Mexico	4.0	India	7.3
4	Japan	4.6	Korea, Rep. of	5.9	India	5.0	Taiwan	3.2	Japan	6.8
5	Taiwan	4.6	China	5.6	China	2.6	China	3.1	Taiwan	5.6
6	Canada	4.3	Canada	4.7	Bulgaria	2.4	Colombia	3.0	China	5.2
7	Turkey	2.2	Kenya	2.4	United Kingdom	2.3	India	2.9	Thailand	2.2
8	Mexico	2.1	Mexico	2.4	Kenya	2.2	Kenya	2.7	Indonesia	2.0
9	Germany	1.6	Thailand	2.0	Nepal	2.2	Hong Kong	2.5	Kenya	1.7
10	Thailand	1.5	Turkey	2.0	Jamaica	2.2	Canada	2.4	Mexico	1.6
11	United Kingdom	1.5	Indonesia	1.9	Taiwan	2.1	Indonesia	2.2	United Kingdom	1.5
12	France	1.4	Nigeria	1.7	Ghana	2.1	Brazil	2.1	Germany	1.5
13	Indonesia	1.4	Pakistan	1.7	Trinidad & Tobago	2.0	Venezuela	2.0	Brazil	1.4
14	Malaysia	1.3	Germany	1.6	Brazil	1.7	Pakistan	1.8	Turkey	1.3
15	Brazil	1.2	Nepal	1.6	Pakistan	1.7	Jamaica	1.8	Colombia	1.3
16	Hong Kong	1.1	United Kingdom	1.4	Germany	1.6	Peru	1.6	Israel	1.0
17	Pakistan	1.1	Brazil	1.3	Nigeria	1.6	Vietnam	1.4	Venezuela	1.0
18	Colombia	1.1	Colombia	1.1	Mexico	1.5	Turkey	1.3	Philippines	0.9
19	Russia	1.0	Russia	1.1	Bahamas	1.5	Nigeria	1.3	Malaysia	0.9
20	Singapore	0.9	Hong Kong	1.1	Turkey	1.1	Poland	1.3	Hong Kong	0.9
TOTAL	354,839		93,687		25,376		75,830		22,777	

Rank	Institution	City	State	Total Int'l Students	Total Enrollment
1	University of Southern California	Los Angeles	CA	6,647	31,606
2	Columbia University	New York	NY	5,362	23,609
3	Purdue University, Main Campus	West Lafayette	IN	5,094	38,847
4	New York University	New York	NY	5,070	38,188
5	University of Texas at Austin	Austin	TX	4,827	51,426
6	University of Illinois at Urbana-Champaign	Champaign	IL	4,769	38,747
7	University of Michigan – Ann Arbor	Ann Arbor	MI	4,583	39,031
8	Boston University	Boston	MA	4,518	29,049
9	University of California – Los Angeles	Los Angeles	CA	4,320	38,598
10	The Ohio State University, Main Campus	Columbus	OH	4,263	50,731
11	Texas A&M University	College Station	TX	3,815	44,813
12	University of Maryland College Park	College Park	MD	3,726	35,329
13	Indiana University at Bloomington	Bloomington	IN	3,715	38,589
14	Penn State University – University Park	University Park	PA	3,693	41,445
15	SUNY at Buffalo	Buffalo	NY	3,664	27,275
16	University of Pennsylvania	Philadelphia	PA	3,557	22,769
17	University of Wisconsin – Madison	Madison	WI	3,435	41,507
18	Harvard University	Cambridge	MA	3,403	19,690
19	Florida International University	Miami	FL	3,397	33,401
20	University of Houston	Houston	TX	3,368	34,699
21	University of Minnesota – Twin Cities	Minneapolis	MN	3,357	49,474
22	Michigan State University	East Lansing	MI	3,277	44,542
23	Wayne State University	Detroit	MI	3,271	33,091
24	University of Florida	Gainesville	FL	3,157	48,673
25	Arizona State University – Tempe Campus	Tempe	AZ	3,038	48,901
26	Stanford University	Stanford	CA	3,007	15,104
27	University of Texas at Arlington	Arlington	TX	2,977	24,979
28	University of Washington	Seattle	WA	2,932	42,707
29	University of Arizona	Tucson	AZ	2,901	38,302
30	Rutgers, The State U. of NJ – New Brunswick	New Brunswick	NJ	2,832	36,000
31	Massachusetts Institute of Technology	Cambridge	MA	2,780	10,992
32	Cornell University	Ithaca	NY	2,724	20,292
33	University of California – Berkeley	Berkeley	CA	2,625	33,076
34	Georgia Institute of Technology	Atlanta	GA	2,617	16,581
35	Carnegie Mellon University	Pittsburgh	PA	2,493	9,756
36	University of Chicago	Chicago	IL	2,470	13,102
37	University of Illinois at Chicago	Chicago	IL	2,439	25,000
38	University of Iowa	Iowa City	IA	2,306	29,745
39	Iowa State University of Science & Technology	Ames	IA	2,302	27,380
40	University of Texas at El Paso	El Paso	TX	2,270	18,542

9 INTERNATIONAL STUDENTS BY INSTITUTIONAL TYPE: TOP 40 DOCTORAL/RESEARCH INSTITUTIONS, 2003/04

Rank	Institution	City	State	Total Int'l Students	Total Enrollment
1	CUNY Bernard M. Baruch College	New York	NY	3,012	15,361
2	San Francisco State University	San Francisco	CA	2,497	29,686
3	California State University – Long Beach	Long Beach	CA	1,934	34,715
4	California State University – Northridge	Northridge	CA	1,601	32,618
5	California State University – Fullerton	Fullerton	CA	1,581	32,545
6	San Jose State University	San Jose	CA	1,529	30,350
7	Hawaii Pacific University	Honolulu	HI	1,517	8,137
8	University of Central Oklahoma	Edmond	OK	1,490	14,174
9	California State University – Hayward	Hayward	CA	1,444	13,627
10	Rochester Institute of Technology	Rochester	NY	1,421	15,334
11	Johnson & Wales University	Providence	RI	1,138	13,432
12	CUNY Hunter College	New York	NY	1,126	20,000
13	NY Institute of Technology – Old Westbury	Old Westbury	NY	1,076	9,683
14	Eastern Michigan University	Ypsilanti	MI	1,033	24,287
15	CUNY City College	New York	NY	1,031	12,550
16	St. Cloud State University	St. Cloud	MN	936	16,313
17	California State University – Los Angeles	Los Angeles	CA	888	20,637
18	CUNY Brooklyn College	Brooklyn	NY	883	15,635
19	University of North Carolina at Charlotte	Charlotte	NC	873	19,605
20	Santa Clara University	Santa Clara	CA	838	8,047
21	California State Polytechnic University – Pomona	Pomona	CA	821	19,804
22	California State University – Fresno	Fresno	CA	818	18,293
23	University of Nebraska at Omaha	Omaha	NE	807	13,997
24	Fairleigh Dickinson U. – Florham & Metropolitan	Teaneck	NJ	802	10,956
25	Montclair State University	Upper Montclair	NJ	789	15,204
26	California State University – San Bernardino	San Bernardino	CA	739	16,000
27	California State University – Sacramento	Sacramento	CA	733	28,375
28	University of Texas at San Antonio	San Antonio	TX	732	22,016
29	Oklahoma City University	Oklahoma City	OK	731	3,668
30	Towson University	Towson	MD	712	17,188
31	Suffolk University	Boston	MA	673	6,236
32	Minnesota State University, Mankato	Mankato	MN	636	14,058
33	University of Houston – Clear Lake	Houston	TX	615	7,753
34	Lamar University	Beaumont	TX	613	10,379
35	Bentley College	Waltham	MA	610	5,648
36	University of Maryland University College	Adelphi	MD	596	24,030
37	Texas State University – San Marcos	San Marcos	TX	541	26,366
38	Western Kentucky University	Bowling Green	KY	525	18,500
39	Seattle University	Seattle	WA	508	6,659
40	University of Texas – Pan American	Edinburg	TX	502	15,914

10 INTERNATIONAL STUDENTS BY INSTITUTIONAL TYPE: TOP 40 MASTER'S INSTITUTIONS, 2003/04

Rank	Institution	City	State	Total Int'l Students	Total Enrollment
1	Brigham Young University – Hawaii	Laie, Oahu	HI	1,150	2,471
2	Fashion Institute of Technology	New York	NY	1,119	7,439
3	Utah Valley State College	Orem	UT	532	23,803
4	University of Dallas	Irving	TX	455	3,266
5	Mount Holyoke College	South Hadley	MA	368	2,087
6	Calvin College	Grand Rapids	MI	357	4,332
7	University of Hawaii at Hilo	Hilo	HI	340	3,040
8	University of Maine at Presque Isle	Presque Isle	ME	323	1,560
9	Florida Memorial College	Miami	FL	311	2,177
10	St. Francis College	Brooklyn	NY	300	2,294
11	Wesleyan University	Middletown	CT	280	3,192
12	Daemen College	Amherst	NY	268	2,205
13	CUNY New York City College of Technology	Brooklyn	NY	267	10,900
13	University of Maine at Fort Kent	Fort Kent	ME	267	778
15	Macalester College	St. Paul	MN	264	1,851
16	University of Houston – Downtown	Houston	TX	262	10,974
17	East-West University	Chicago	IL	241	1,113
18	Smith College	Northampton	MA	236	2,862
19	CUNY York College	Jamaica	NY	225	5,935
20	Metropolitan State College of Denver	Denver	CO	209	19,390
21	Middlebury College	Middlebury	VT	200	2,297
21	Oberlin College	Oberlin	OH	200	2,848
23	Wellesley College	Wellesley	MA	194	2,248
24	Ohio Wesleyan University	Delaware	OH	192	1,929
25	Lakeland College	Sheboygan	WI	189	3,948
25	Ramapo College of New Jersey	Mahwah	NJ	188	5,631
27	Concordia College – Moorhead	Moorhead	MN	171	2,856
27	Willamette University	Salem	OR	171	2,510
29	Franklin & Marshall College	Lancaster	PA	169	1,929
30	Coastal Carolina University	Conway	SC	167	6,780
31	Grinnell College	Grinnell	IA	164	1,485
32	College of Saint Benedict/Saint John's University	Collegeville	MN	161	2,011
33	Colgate University	Hamilton	NY	159	2,707
34	Lawrence University	Appleton	WI	158	1,325
35	Dordt College	Sioux Center	IA	157	1,287
35	Drew University	Madison	NJ	157	2,521
35	Southwest Minnesota State University	Marshall	MN	157	5,056
38	Bethune Cookman College	Daytona Beach	FL	156	2,794
39	CUNY Medgar Evers College	Brooklyn	NY	154	5,000
40	Williams College	Williamstown	MA	153	2,080

11 INTERNATIONAL STUDENTS BY INSTITUTIONAL TYPE: TOP 40 BACCALAUREATE INSTITUTIONS, 2003/04

Rank	Institution	City	State	Total Int'l Students	Total Enrollment
1	Santa Monica College	Santa Monica	CA	2,921	23,873
2	Houston Community College System	Houston	TX	2,547	58,210
3	De Anza College	Cupertino	CA	2,340	26,000
4	Miami-Dade Community College	Miami	FL	2,219	59,868
5	Northern Virginia Community College	Annandale	VA	2,176	38,097
6	CUNY Borough of Manhattan Community College	New York	NY	1,863	17,540
7	CUNY Queensborough Community College	Bayside	NY	1,706	11,068
8	Montgomery College	Rockville	MD	1,621	21,671
9	Foothill College	Los Altos Hills	CA	1,410	17,300
10	City College of San Francisco	San Francisco	CA	1,163	66,133
11	Nassau Community College	Garden City	NY	1,049	19,713
12	North Lake College	Irving	TX	1,046	14,136
13	Austin Community College	Austin	TX	996	29,156
14	Pasadena City College	Pasadena	CA	969	25,549
15	CUNY La Guardia Community College	Long Island City	NY	938	12,600
16	Los Angeles City College	Los Angeles	CA	899	15,651
17	Oakland Community College	Bloomington Hills	MI	875	15,722
18	Richland College	Dallas	TX	841	13,880
19	Broward Community College	Fort Lauderdale	FL	828	34,377
20	El Camino College	Torrance	CA	796	26,500
21	Diablo Valley College	Pleasant Hill	CA	713	21,061
22	Georgia Perimeter College	Clarkston	GA	685	19,878
23	Collin County Community College District	McKinney	TX	680	16,574
24	CUNY Kingsborough Community College	Brooklyn	NY	643	14,944
24	Grossmont College	El Cajon	CA	643	17,096
26	Orange Coast College	Costa Mesa	CA	639	22,594
26	Santa Ana College – Rancho Santiago C.C. Dist.	Santa Ana	CA	639	34,432
28	Quincy College	Quincy	MA	638	4,496
29	Seattle Central Community College	Seattle	WA	612	10,721
30	North Harris Montgomery Community College Dist.	Houston	TX	602	34,306
31	Community College of Southern Nevada	Las Vegas	NV	597	31,000
32	Bergen Community College	Paramus	NJ	573	13,253
33	Seminole Community College	Sanford	FL	556	19,052
34	Phoenix College	Phoenix	AZ	555	13,150
35	Edmonds Community College	Lynnwood	WA	551	11,244
36	Pima Community College	Tucson	AZ	549	29,350
37	Bellevue Community College	Bellevue	WA	541	21,694
38	Glendale Community College	Glendale	CA	540	15,800
39	Bunker Hill Community College	Boston	MA	515	7,397
40	Shoreline Community College	Seattle	WA	505	8,200

12   INTERNATIONAL STUDENTS BY INSTITUTIONAL TYPE: TOP 40 ASSOCIATE'S INSTITUTIONS, 2003/04

Rank	Institution	City	State	Total Int'l Students	Total Enrollment
1	Academy of Art College	San Francisco	CA	1,685	6,719
2	D'Youville College	Buffalo	NY	1,161	2,490
3	Berklee College of Music	Boston	MA	955	3,799
4	Pratt Institute	Brooklyn	NY	700	5,275
5	Southern Polytechnic State University	Marietta	GA	613	3,770
6	Southern New Hampshire University	Manchester	NH	602	6,615
7	School of Visual Arts	New York	NY	595	5,328
8	Babson College	Babson Park	MA	582	3,342
9	Savannah College of Art and Design	Savannah	GA	562	6,207
10	Franklin University	Columbus	OH	486	6,286
11	Thunderbird, Garvin Grad. School of Int'l Mgmt.	Glendale	AZ	482	938
12	Golden Gate University	San Francisco	CA	462	4,299
13	Fuller Theological Seminary	Pasadena	CA	389	1,792
14	School of the Art Institute of Chicago	Chicago	IL	369	2,462
15	Naval Postgraduate School	Monterey	CA	346	1,285
16	Colorado School of Mines	Golden	CO	343	3,364
17	University of Texas Health Science Ctr. at Houston	Houston	TX	329	3,417
18	Goldey-Beacom College	Wilmington	DE	327	1,416
19	Rhode Island School of Design	Providence	RI	274	2,204
20	University of Tennessee, Health Science Center	Memphis	TN	250	2,039
21	Southwestern Baptist Theological Seminary	Fort Worth	TX	246	2,887
22	Manhattan School of Music	New York	NY	243	819
23	Arizona State University – East Campus	Mesa	AZ	232	3,551
24	The Juilliard School	New York	NY	228	850
25	School of Advanced Int'l Studies, The Johns Hopkins U.	Washington	DC	222	669
26	Miami International University of Art & Design	Miami	FL	215	1,289
27	Art Center College of Design	Pasadena	CA	210	1,500
28	University of Medicine & Dentistry of New Jersey	Newark	NJ	205	4,949
29	Tufts U., Fletcher School of Law & Diplomacy	Medford	MA	202	453
30	Northwood University, Michigan	Midland	MI	201	2,052
31	Baylor College of Medicine	Houston	TX	193	1,287
32	Davenport University	Grand Rapids	MI	192	14,620
33	Palmer College of Chiropractic	Davenport	IA	180	1,750
34	Oregon Health & Science University	Beaverton	OR	171	2,454
35	Catholic Theological Union	Chicago	IL	160	502
36	California Institute of the Arts	Valencia	CA	158	1,273
37	Peabody Institute of The Johns Hopkins University	Baltimore	MD	155	639
38	Trinity Evangelical Divinity School	Deerfield	IL	153	1,351
39	South Dakota School of Mines & Technology	Rapid City	SD	146	2,454
40	Life University, College of Chiropractic	Marietta	GA	144	1,200

13   **INTERNATIONAL STUDENTS BY INSTITUTIONAL TYPE: TOP 40 SPECIALIZED INSTITUTIONS, 2003/04**

Rank	Institution	City	State	Total Int'l Students	Total Enrollment
1	University of Southern California	Los Angeles	CA	6,647	31,606
2	Columbia University	New York	NY	5,362	23,609
3	Purdue University, Main Campus	West Lafayette	IN	5,094	38,847
4	New York University	New York	NY	5,070	38,188
5	University of Texas at Austin	Austin	TX	4,827	51,426
6	University of Illinois at Urbana-Champaign	Champaign	IL	4,769	38,747
7	University of Michigan – Ann Arbor	Ann Arbor	MI	4,583	39,031
8	Boston University	Boston	MA	4,518	29,049
9	University of California – Los Angeles	Los Angeles	CA	4,320	38,598
10	The Ohio State University, Main Campus	Columbus	OH	4,263	50,731
11	Texas A&M University	College Station	TX	3,815	44,813
12	University of Maryland College Park	College Park	MD	3,726	35,329
13	Indiana University at Bloomington	Bloomington	IN	3,715	38,589
14	Penn State University – University Park	University Park	PA	3,693	41,445
15	SUNY at Buffalo	Buffalo	NY	3,664	27,275
16	University of Pennsylvania	Philadelphia	PA	3,557	22,769
17	University of Wisconsin – Madison	Madison	WI	3,435	41,507
18	Harvard University	Cambridge	MA	3,403	19,690
19	Florida International University	Miami	FL	3,397	33,401
20	University of Houston	Houston	TX	3,368	34,699
21	University of Minnesota – Twin Cities	Minneapolis	MN	3,357	49,474
22	Michigan State University	East Lansing	MI	3,277	44,542
23	Wayne State University	Detroit	MI	3,271	33,091
24	University of Florida	Gainesville	FL	3,157	48,673
25	Arizona State University – Tempe Campus	Tempe	AZ	3,038	48,901
26	CUNY Bernard M. Baruch College	New York	NY	3,012	15,361
27	Stanford University	Stanford	CA	3,007	15,104
28	University of Texas at Arlington	Arlington	TX	2,977	24,979
29	University of Washington	Seattle	WA	2,932	42,707
30	Santa Monica College	Santa Monica	CA	2,921	23,873
31	University of Arizona	Tucson	AZ	2,901	38,302
32	Rutgers, The State U. of NJ – New Brunswick	New Brunswick	NJ	2,832	36,000
33	Massachusetts Institute of Technology	Cambridge	MA	2,780	10,992
34	Cornell University	Ithaca	NY	2,724	20,292
35	University of California – Berkeley	Berkeley	CA	2,625	33,076
36	Georgia Institute of Technology	Atlanta	GA	2,617	16,581
37	Houston Community College System	Houston	TX	2,547	58,210
38	San Francisco State University	San Francisco	CA	2,497	29,686
39	Carnegie Mellon University	Pittsburgh	PA	2,493	9,756
40	University of Chicago	Chicago	IL	2,470	13,102
41	University of Illinois at Chicago	Chicago	IL	2,439	25,000
42	De Anza College	Cupertino	CA	2,340	26,000
43	University of Iowa	Iowa City	IA	2,306	29,745
44	Iowa State University of Science & Technology	Ames	IA	2,302	27,380
45	University of Texas at El Paso	El Paso	TX	2,270	18,542

14 **INSTITUTIONS WITH 1,000 OR MORE INTERNATIONAL STUDENTS:**
RANKED BY INTERNATIONAL STUDENT TOTAL, 2003/04

Rank	Institution	City	State	Total Int'l Students	Total Enrollment
46	Syracuse University	Syracuse	NY	2,233	18,590
47	Miami-Dade Community College	Miami	FL	2,219	59,868
48	Northern Virginia Community College	Annandale	VA	2,176	38,097
49	Oklahoma State University, Main Campus	Stillwater	OK	2,168	23,571
50	University of North Texas	Denton	TX	2,142	32,419
51	Virginia Polytechnic Institute & State University	Blacksburg	VA	2,118	28,027
52	Temple University	Philadelphia	PA	2,115	33,286
53	University of South Florida	Tampa	FL	2,112	42,000
54	Northwestern University	Evanston	IL	2,102	17,363
55	Northeastern University	Boston	MA	2,101	24,501
56	Illinois Institute of Technology	Chicago	IL	2,058	6,167
57	University of Cincinnati	Cincinnati	OH	2,030	33,823
58	Brigham Young University	Provo	UT	2,024	32,408
59	SUNY at Stony Brook	Stony Brook	NY	2,019	22,344
60	The University of Texas at Dallas	Richardson	TX	1,973	13,038
61	California State University – Long Beach	Long Beach	CA	1,934	34,715
62	George Washington University	Washington	DC	1,902	23,417
63	George Mason University	Fairfax	VA	1,877	29,325
64	CUNY Borough of Manhattan Community College	New York	NY	1,863	17,540
65	University of Connecticut	Storrs	CT	1,817	26,629
66	Louisiana State University	Baton Rouge	LA	1,813	31,234
67	University of California – San Diego	La Jolla	CA	1,811	26,677
68	University of Oklahoma – Norman	Norman	OK	1,799	26,911
69	Yale University	New Haven	CT	1,765	11,385
70	Georgia State University	Atlanta	GA	1,764	27,451
71	University of Pittsburgh, Main Campus	Pittsburgh	PA	1,734	26,795
72	Western Michigan University	Kalamazoo	MI	1,726	29,179
73	University of California – Davis	Davis	CA	1,712	29,087
74	CUNY Queensborough Community College	Bayside	NY	1,706	11,068
75	Southern Illinois University Carbondale	Carbondale	IL	1,704	21,387
76	Academy of Art University	San Francisco	CA	1,685	6,719
77	New School University	New York	NY	1,672	8,337
78	University of Hawaii at Manoa	Honolulu	HI	1,657	19,401
79	University of Kansas	Lawrence	KS	1,639	26,814
80	University of Miami	Coral Gables	FL	1,632	15,248
81	Montgomery College	Rockville	MD	1,621	21,671
82	University of Oregon	Eugene	OR	1,610	20,033
83	University of Massachusetts at Amherst	Amherst	MA	1,602	24,062
84	California State University – Northridge	Northridge	CA	1,601	32,618
85	California State University – Fullerton	Fullerton	CA	1,581	32,545
85	Duke University & Medical Center	Durham	NC	1,581	13,514
87	University of Utah	Salt Lake City	UT	1,562	27,000
88	University of California – Irvine	Irvine	CA	1,561	24,874
88	Drexel University	Philadelphia	PA	1,561	17,000
90	San Jose State University	San Jose	CA	1,529	30,350

14 (cont'd) INSTITUTIONS WITH 1,000 OR MORE INTERNATIONAL STUDENTS: RANKED BY INTERNATIONAL STUDENT TOTAL, 2003/04

Rank	Institution	City	State	Total Int'l Students	Total Enrollment
91	Georgetown University	Washington	DC	1,517	13,164
91	Hawaii Pacific University	Honolulu	HI	1,517	8,137
93	Washington University	St. Louis	MO	1,508	12,088
94	North Carolina State University	Raleigh	NC	1,505	29,637
95	University of Central Oklahoma	Edmond	OK	1,490	14,174
96	University of Delaware	Newark	DE	1,485	20,501
97	San Diego State University	San Diego	CA	1,464	33,676
98	University of Virginia, Main Campus	Charlottesville	VA	1,452	19,856
99	California State University – Hayward	Hayward	CA	1,444	13,627
99	Florida Atlantic University	Boca Raton	FL	1,444	25,018
101	University of Missouri – Columbia	Columbia	MO	1,427	26,805
101	University of North Carolina at Chapel Hill	Chapel Hill	NC	1,427	26,359
103	Rochester Institute of Technology	Rochester	NY	1,421	15,334
104	Foothill College	Los Altos Hills	CA	1,410	17,300
105	University of Nebraska – Lincoln	Lincoln	NE	1,406	22,559
106	University of Georgia	Athens	GA	1,405	33,878
107	West Virginia University	Morgantown	WV	1,403	24,260
108	University of Kentucky	Lexington	KY	1,372	25,397
109	University of Central Florida	Orlando	FL	1,355	41,102
110	Wichita State University	Wichita	KS	1,333	14,896
111	New Jersey Institute of Technology	Newark	NJ	1,260	8,770
112	Washington State University	Pullman	WA	1,250	22,861
113	Binghamton University – SUNY	Binghamton	NY	1,241	13,865
114	Howard University	Washington	DC	1,229	11,256
115	Ohio University, Main Campus	Athens	OH	1,220	19,959
116	Princeton University	Princeton	NJ	1,217	6,685
117	University of Nevada, Las Vegas	Las Vegas	NV	1,211	26,393
118	University of Bridgeport	Bridgeport	CT	1,208	3,374
119	Case Western Reserve University	Cleveland	OH	1,186	9,097
120	Texas Tech University	Lubbock	TX	1,182	28,549
121	City College of San Francisco	San Francisco	CA	1,163	66,133
121	University of South Carolina – Columbia	Columbia	SC	1,163	25,288
123	D'Youville College	Buffalo	NY	1,161	2,490
124	University of Rochester	Rochester	NY	1,156	8,662
125	Brigham Young University – Hawaii	Laie, Oahu	HI	1,150	2,471
126	Johnson & Wales University	Providence	RI	1,138	13,432
127	Old Dominion University	Norfolk	VA	1,127	20,802
128	CUNY Hunter College	New York	NY	1,126	20,000
129	Fashion Institute of Technology – SUNY	New York	NY	1,119	7,439
130	Brown University	Providence	RI	1,111	7,892
131	University of Colorado at Boulder	Boulder	CO	1,082	27,000
132	American University	Washington	DC	1,080	11,748
133	NY Institute of Technology – Old Westbury	Old Westbury	NY	1,076	9,683
134	Portland State University	Portland	OR	1,073	20,110
135	University of Alabama at Birmingham	Birmingham	AL	1,071	16,357

14 (cont'd) INSTITUTIONS WITH 1,000 OR MORE INTERNATIONAL STUDENTS:
RANKED BY INTERNATIONAL STUDENT TOTAL, 2003/04

Rank	Institution	City	State	Total Int'l Students	Total Enrollment
136	Florida State University	Tallahassee	FL	1,069	37,328
137	Oregon State University	Corvallis	OR	1,063	18,979
138	Nassau Community College	Garden City	NY	1,049	19,713
139	North Lake College	Irving	TX	1,046	14,136
140	Tulane University	New Orleans	LA	1,043	11,500
141	Eastern Michigan University	Ypsilanti	MI	1,033	24,287
142	CUNY City College	New York	NY	1,031	12,550
143	The University of Memphis	Memphis	TN	1,018	19,797
144	University of Tennessee at Knoxville	Knoxville	TN	1,014	26,000
145	University of California – Santa Barbara	Santa Barbara	CA	1,004	20,847
146	University of California – Riverside	Riverside	CA	1,002	15,934
147	Rensselaer Polytechnic Institute	Troy	NY	1,001	6,656
148	Kansas State University	Manhattan	KS	1,000	23,050

14 (cont'd) INSTITUTIONS WITH 1,000 OR MORE INTERNATIONAL STUDENTS: RANKED BY INTERNATIONAL STUDENT TOTAL, 2003/04

Field of Study	2002/03 Int'l Students	2003/04 Int'l Students	2003/04 % of Total	% Change
Agriculture, Total	**6,763**	**7,293**	**1.3**	**7.8**
Agricultural Sciences	2,859	2,867	0.5	0.3
Agribusiness and Agricultural Production	1,931	2,539	0.4	31.5
Natural Resources and Conservation *	1,973	1,886	0.3	-4.4
Business and Management, Total	**114,777**	**108,788**	**19.0**	**-5.2**
Business and Management, General	108,748	103,935	18.2	-4.4
Marketing and Distribution	5,242	3,974	0.7	-24.2
Consumer, Personal, and Miscellaneous Services	787	879	0.2	11.7
Education	**16,004**	**15,909**	**2.8**	**-0.6**
Engineering, Total	**96,545**	**95,221**	**16.6**	**-1.4**
Engineering, General	88,809	87,528	15.3	-1.4
Engineering-Related Technologies	5,781	5,920	1.0	2.4
Transportation and Material Moving	1,083	1,012	0.2	-6.6
Mechanics and Repairers	426	486	0.1	14.1
Construction Trades	306	184	0.0	-39.9
Precision Production	140	90	0.0	-35.7
Fine and Applied Arts, Total	**31,018**	**31,882**	**5.6**	**2.8**
Visual and Performing Arts	24,306	25,204	4.4	3.7

15 INTERNATIONAL STUDENTS BY FIELD OF STUDY, 2002/03 & 2003/04

Field of Study	2002/03 Int'l Students	2003/04 Int'l Students	2003/04 % of Total	% Change
Architecture and Environmental Design	6,712	6,678	1.2	-0.5
Health Professions	**28,120**	**25,749**	**4.5**	**-8.4**
Humanities, Total	**19,153**	**16,622**	**2.9**	**-13.2**
Letters	5,912	4,841	0.8	-18.1
Foreign Languages	6,845	5,366	0.9	-21.6
Theology	4,406	4,172	0.7	-5.3
Philosophy and Religion	1,990	2,243	0.4	12.7
Mathematics and Computer Sciences, Total	**71,926**	**67,693**	**11.8**	**-5.9**
Computer and Information Sciences	61,857	57,739	10.1	-6.7
Mathematics	10,069	9,954	1.7	-1.1
Physical and Life Sciences, Total	**43,549**	**44,607**	**7.8**	**2.4**
Physical Sciences	19,484	19,603	3.4	0.6
Life Sciences	22,960	23,290	4.1	1.4
Science Technologies	1,105	1,714	0.3	55.1
Social Sciences, Total	**45,978**	**54,153**	**9.5**	**17.8**
Social Sciences, General	26,775	34,101	6.0	27.4
Psychology	8,522	8,352	1.5	-2.0
Public Administration and Social Service **	4,814	5,372	0.9	11.6
Area and Ethnic Studies	2304	2639	0.5	14.5
Security and Protective Services ***	723	817	0.1	13.0
Parks and Recreation	2,840	2,872	0.5	1.1
Other, Total	**58,473**	**60,273**	**10.5**	**3.1**
Liberal/General Studies	29,972	32,007	5.6	6.8
Communications and Journalism +	10,249	9,104	1.6	-11.2
Law	6,411	6,222	1.1	-2.9
Multi/Interdisciplinary Studies	5,058	7,057	1.2	39.5
Family and Consumer Sciences/Human Sciences +*	2,458	2,157	0.4	-12.2
Library and Archival Sciences	901	742	0.1	-17.6
Vocational Home Economics	918	644	0.1	-29.8
Communication Technologies	2,477	2,335	0.4	-5.7
Military Technologies	29	5	0.0	-82.8
Intensive English Language	**17,620**	**15,006**	**2.6**	**-14.8**
Undeclared	**36,395**	**29,313**	**5.1**	**-19.5**
TOTAL	**586,323**	**572,509**	**100.0**	**-2.4**

* formerly Conservation and Renewable Natural Resources   ** formerly Public Administration
*** formerly Protective Services   + formerly Communications   +* formerly Home Economics

15   (cont'd) INTERNATIONAL STUDENTS BY FIELD OF STUDY, 2002/03 & 2003/04

Doctoral/Research Institutions	% Enrollment
Engineering	22.4
Business & Management	15.7
Mathematics & Computer Sciences	12.5
Social Sciences	10.9
Physical & Life Sciences	9.6
Other	8.2
Fine & Applied Arts	4.2
Health Professions	3.9
Undeclared	3.8
Humanities	2.6
Education	2.5
Intensive English Language	1.9
Agriculture	1.7

Master's Institutions	% Enrollment
Business & Management	31.8
Mathematics & Computer Sciences	13.4
Engineering	8.5
Social Sciences	8.5
Other	8.1
Physical & Life Sciences	5.1
Undeclared	5.1
Fine & Applied Arts	5.0
Intensive English Language	4.0
Education	3.7
Health Professions	3.5
Humanities	2.8
Agriculture	0.5

Baccalaureate Institutions	% Enrollment
Business & Management	23.0
Undeclared	13.9
Social Sciences	13.8
Other	13.0
Mathematics & Computer Sciences	8.6
Physical & Life Sciences	7.0
Education	5.0
Fine & Applied Arts	4.1
Humanities	4.0
Engineering	2.9
Intensive English Language	2.1
Health Professions	2.0
Agriculture	0.5

Associate's Institutions	% Enrollment
Other	27.0
Business & Management	20.1
Undeclared	10.4
Mathematics & Computer Sciences	9.9
Health Professions	8.1
Engineering	5.4
Fine & Applied Arts	5.0
Intensive English Language	4.9
Social Sciences	3.1
Physical & Life Sciences	3.0
Education	1.6
Humanities	1.0
Agriculture	0.5

Specialized Institutions	% Enrollment
Fine & Applied Arts	33.5
Business & Management	14.3
Humanities	12.5
Health Professions	9.9
Engineering	5.7
Social Sciences	5.0
Physical & Life Sciences	5.0
Education	4.8
Mathematics & Computer Sciences	3.7
Other	2.8
Intensive English Language	1.7
Undeclared	1.0
Agriculture	0.1

16 FIELDS OF STUDY BY INSTITUTIONAL TYPE, 2003/04

Academic Level	2002/03 Int'l Students	2002/03 % of Total	2003/04 Int'l Students	2003/04 % of Total	% Change
Associate's	**72,494**	**12.4**	**69,541**	**12.1**	**-4.1**
Bachelor's	**187,609**	**32.0**	**178,659**	**31.2**	**-4.8**
Freshman	36,521	6.2	32,489	5.7	-11.0
Sophomore	31,162	5.3	28,265	4.9	-9.3
Junior	37,249	6.4	36,312	6.3	-2.5
Senior	49,437	8.4	48,281	8.4	-2.3
Unspecified	33,240	5.7	33,312	5.8	0.2
Graduate	**267,876**	**45.7**	**274,310**	**47.9**	**2.4**
Master's	138,634	23.6	142,271	24.9	2.6
Doctoral	92,203	15.7	100,092	17.5	8.6
Professional Training	7,796	1.3	8,212	1.4	5.3
Unspecified	29,243	5.0	23,735	4.1	-18.8
Other	**58,344**	**10.0**	**49,999**	**8.7**	**-14.3**
Practical Training	27,793	4.7	29,340	5.1	5.6
Non-Degree	13,695	2.3	10,435	1.8	-23.8
Intensive English Language	16,856	2.9	10,224	1.8	-39.3
TOTAL	**586,323**	**100.0**	**572,509**	**100.0**	**-2.4**

17   INTERNATIONAL STUDENTS BY ACADEMIC LEVEL, 2002/03 & 2003/04

Year	Under-graduate	Graduate	Other
1954/55	19,101	12,118	3,012
1959/60	25,164	18,910	4,412
1964/65	38,130	35,096	8,774
1969/70	63,296	59,112	12,551
1975/76	95,949	83,395	18,073
1979/80	172,378	94,207	19,758
1984/85	197,741	122,476	21,895
1987/88	176,669	156,366	23,152
1988/89	172,551	165,590	28,209
1989/90	184,527	169,827	32,495
1990/91	189,900	182,130	35,500
1991/92	197,070	191,330	31,190
1992/93	210,080	193,330	35,210
1993/94	213,610	201,030	35,110
1994/95	221,500	191,738	39,396
1995/96	218,620	190,092	45,075
1996/97	218,743	190,244	48,997
1997/98	223,276	207,510	50,494
1998/99	235,802	211,426	43,706
1999/00	237,211	218,219	59,293
2000/01	254,429	238,497	54,941
2001/02	261,079	264,749	57,168
2002/03	260,103	267,876	58,344
2003/04	248,200	274,310	49,999

18 INTERNATIONAL STUDENTS BY ACADEMIC LEVEL, SELECTED YEARS 1954/55 – 2003/04

Characteristic	% Under-graduate	% Graduate	% Other	Characteristic	% Under-graduate	% Graduate	% Other
Sex				U.S. Private Sponsor	2.8	1.5	2.0
Male	51.5	60.2	52.2	Foreign Private Sponsor	2.6	1.7	1.3
Female	48.5	39.8	47.8	Current Employment	0.2	0.5	0.8
				International Organization	0.3	1.4	13.9
Marital Status				Other Sources	0.0	0.0	0.0
Single	93.0	77.1	85.9				
Married	7.0	22.9	14.1	**Field of Study**			
				Agriculture	0.6	1.9	0.5
Enrollment Status				Business & Management	21.7	17.7	12.3
Full-Time	89.5	86.5	84.4	Education	1.5	4.2	1.1
Part-Time	10.5	13.5	15.6	Engineering	9.2	23.6	7.7
				Fine & Applied Arts	6.8	4.6	3.7
Visa Type				Health Professions	5.0	5.0	2.6
F Visa	86.0	86.5	78.7	Humanities	1.9	4.2	3.0
J Visa	3.1	5.6	10.4	Math & Computer Sciences	12.0	11.9	5.6
M Visa	0.2	0.0	0.2	Physical & Life Sciences	5.9	11.1	2.5
Other Visa	10.7	7.8	10.7	Social Sciences	13.4	8.9	3.6
				Other	14.4	5.9	5.8
Primary Source of Funds				Intensive English	0.6	0.1	34.1
Personal & Family	81.7	51.4	69.7	Undeclared	7.0	0.9	17.7
U.S. College or University	10.2	40.5	7.8				
Home Gov't/University	2.0	2.2	4.1	**NUMBER OF STUDENTS**	**248,200**	**274,310**	**49,999**
U.S. Government	0.3	0.7	0.3				

19   PERSONAL AND ACADEMIC CHARACTERISTICS OF INTERNATIONAL STUDENTS BY ACADEMIC LEVEL, 2003/04

Year	% Male	% Female	% Single	% F Visa	% J Visa	% Other Visa	% Refugee*	Int'l Students
1976/77	69.2	30.8	73.7	75.0	10.4	7.3	7.3	203,068
1977/78	75.0	25.0	77.4	78.8	9.3	6.9	5.0	235,509
1978/79	74.1	25.9	74.7	80.7	9.8	5.7	3.8	263,938
1979/80	72.4	27.6	78.6	82.0	7.6	6.4	4.0	286,343
1980/81	71.7	28.3	80.1	82.9	6.7	5.6	4.8	311,882
1981/82	71.0	29.0	79.3	84.3	6.8	4.9	4.0	326,299
1982/83	70.9	29.1	80.1	84.0	7.2	5.2	3.6	336,985
1983/84	70.6	29.4	80.1	83.2	8.2	5.2	3.4	338,894
1984/85	69.8	30.2	80.4	83.5	8.4	5.1	3.0	342,113
1985/86	70.7	29.3	80.0	81.5	9.2	5.7	3.6	343,777
1986/87	68.9	31.1	79.7	81.0	11.0	5.2	2.8	349,609
1987/88	67.7	32.3	79.8	79.4	12.1	6.1	2.3	356,187
1988/89	66.5	33.5	80.9	79.0	12.5	6.5	2.0	366,354
1989/90	66.1	33.9	80.1	78.5	12.7	6.4	2.4	386,851
1990/91	64.0	36.0	78.5	80.6	11.0	6.4	2.0	407,529
1991/92	63.7	36.3	80.7	84.6	9.5	6.0	.	419,585
1992/93	63.0	37.0	82.5	85.5	8.5	6.1	.	438,618
1993/94	62.1	37.9	83.1	86.4	7.7	5.9	.	449,749
1994/95	60.9	39.1	83.4	85.8	7.7	6.4	.	452,635
1995/96	58.9	41.1	82.6	84.9	7.7	7.3	.	453,787
1996/97	59.0	41.0	84.4	85.6	6.8	7.6	.	457,984
1997/98	58.1	41.9	83.6	86.8	6.7	6.5	.	481,280
1998/99	58.0	42.0	85.2	87.3	6.3	6.4	.	490,933
1999/00	57.5	42.5	84.2	85.6	5.8	8.6	.	514,723
2000/01	57.1	42.9	84.7	85.8	5.8	8.4	.	547,867
2001/02	57.0	43.0	86.0	86.2	5.1	8.7	.	582,996
2002/03	56.2	43.8	85.0	86.0	4.9	9.1	.	586,323
2003/04	55.8	44.2	85.3	85.7	5.1	9.2		572,509

* After 1990, IIE ceased to collect data on refugee students.

20   PERSONAL CHARACTERISTICS OF INTERNATIONAL STUDENTS, 1976/77 – 2003/04

STUDY ABROAD

IN THIS SECTION

PERCENT OF U.S. STUDY ABROAD STUDENTS

Host Region	1993/94	1994/95	1995/96	1996/97	1997/98	1998/99	1999/00	2000/01	2001/02	2002/03
Africa	1.9	2.2	2.3	2.6	2.7	2.8	2.8	2.9	2.9	2.7
Asia	6.5	6.4	6.4	6.1	6.0	6.0	6.2	6.0	6.8	5.5
Europe	67.4	65.5	64.8	64.5	63.7	62.7	62.4	63.1	62.6	63.5
Latin America	13.4	13.7	15.4	15.3	15.6	15.0	14.0	14.5	14.5	15.0
Middle East	2.8	3.3	2.1	1.9	2.0	2.8	2.9	1.1	0.8	0.4
North America*	0.7	0.7	0.7	0.7	0.9	0.7	0.9	0.7	0.8	0.7
Oceania	3.4	4.3	4.4	4.4	4.4	4.9	5.0	6.0	6.8	7.2
Multiple Regions	3.8	3.8	4.0	4.6	4.8	5.2	5.8	5.6	4.9	5.0
Students Reported	**76,302**	**84,403**	**89,242**	**99,448**	**113,959**	**129,770**	**143,590**	**154,168**	**160,920**	**174,629**

* Includes Antarctica in 2002/03

21   HOST REGIONS OF U.S. STUDY ABROAD STUDENTS, 1993/94 – 2002/03

Destination	2001/02	2002/03	% Change	Destination	2001/02	2002/03	% Change
AFRICA	**4,633**	**4,827**	**4.2**	**North Africa**	**431**	**495**	**14.8**
Africa, Unspecified	59	1	-98.3	Canary Islands	0	0	-
				Egypt	241	303	25.7
East Africa	**1,291**	**1,209**	**-6.4**	Morocco	170	191	12.4
Angola	1	0	-100.0	Western Sahara	0	0	-
Eritrea	0	12	-	Tunisia	20	0	-100.0
Ethiopia	30	26	-13.3	North Africa, Unspecified	0	1	-
Kenya	720	625	-13.2				
Madagascar	84	15	-82.1	**Southern Africa**	**1,557**	**1,811**	**16.3**
Malawi	9	9	0.0	Botswana	36	42	16.7
Mauritius	1	1	0.0	Lesotho	19	34	78.9
Mozambique	20	29	45.0	Namibia	38	120	215.8
Reunion	1	0	-100.0	South Africa	1,456	1,594	9.5
Rwanda	1	6	500.0	Swaziland	4	21	425.0
Tanzania	293	347	18.4	Southern Africa, Unspec.	4	0	-100.0
Uganda	76	85	11.8				
Zambia	15	24	60.0	**West Africa**	**1,239**	**1,234**	**-0.4**
Zimbabwe	40	29	-27.5	Benin	22	14	-36.4
East Africa, Unspecified	0	1	-	Burkina Faso	33	7	-78.8
				Côte d'Ivoire	21	0	-100.0
Central Africa	**56**	**77**	**37.5**	Gambia	35	22	-37.1
Cameroon	51	66	29.4	Ghana	821	805	-1.9
Central African Republic	0	0	-	Guinea	10	0	-100.0
Chad	0	0	-	Liberia	0	1	-
Congo	2	1	-50.0	Mali	44	31	-29.5
Equatorial Guinea	2	7	250.0	Mauritania	1	4	300.0
Gabon	1	3	200.0	Niger	24	23	-4.2

22   HOST REGIONS AND DESTINATIONS OF U.S. STUDY ABROAD STUDENTS, 2001/02 & 2002/03

Destination	2001/02	2002/03	% Change	Destination	2001/02	2002/03	% Change
Nigeria	10	24	140.0	Armenia	1	3	200.0
Senegal	211	286	35.5	Azerbaijan	1	1	0.0
Sierra Leone	0	7	-	Belarus	13	12	-7.7
Togo	7	7	0.0	Bosnia & Herzegovina	2	15	650.0
West Africa, Unspecified	0	3	-	Bulgaria	12	36	200.0
				Croatia	45	41	-8.9
ASIA	**10,901**	**9,751**	**-10.5**	Czech Republic	1,659	1,997	20.4
Asia, Unspecified	90	0	-100.0	Estonia	9	15	66.7
				Georgia	1	4	300.0
East Asia	**8,419**	**7,322**	**-13.0**	Hungary	452	562	24.3
China	3,911	2,493	-36.3	Latvia	21	4	-81.0
Hong Kong	501	458	-8.6	Lithuania	53	16	-69.8
Japan	3,168	3,457	9.1	Macedonia	0	15	-
Korea, Republic of	631	739	17.1	Moldova	0	4	-
Macao	2	0	-100.0	Poland	378	426	12.7
Mongolia	33	27	-18.2	Romania	57	97	70.2
Taiwan	173	148	-14.5	Russia	1,269	1,521	19.9
				Slovakia	5	29	480.0
South/Central Asia	**916**	**961**	**4.9**	Slovenia	29	26	-10.3
Afghanistan	1	2	100.0	Ukraine	53	123	132.1
Bangladesh	4	21	425.0	Yugoslavia, Former	55	64	16.4
Bhutan	13	1	-92.3	Eastern Europe, Unspec.	35	0	-100.0
India	627	703	12.1				
Kazakhstan	1	2	100.0	**Western Europe**	**96,304**	**104,890**	**8.9**
Kyrgyzstan	0	2	-	Austria	2,180	2,798	28.3
Nepal	214	142	-33.6	Belgium	867	890	2.7
Pakistan	9	9	0.0	Denmark	908	1,127	24.1
Sri Lanka	46	72	56.5	Finland	169	272	60.9
Tajikistan	1	1	0.0	France	12,274	13,080	6.6
Uzbekistan	0	6	-	Germany	4,856	5,587	15.1
				Gibraltar	0	0	-
Southeast Asia	**1,476**	**1,468**	**-0.5**	Greece	1,856	2,011	8.4
Cambodia	10	12	20.0	Iceland	164	134	-18.3
East Timor	1	0	-100.0	Ireland	4,375	4,892	11.8
Indonesia	52	26	-50.0	Italy	17,169	18,936	10.3
Laos	1	2	100.0	Liechtenstein	2	1	-50.0
Malaysia	25	47	88.0	Luxembourg	359	343	-4.5
Myanmar	0	1	-	Malta	101	67	-33.7
Philippines	102	124	21.6	Monaco	0	10	-
Singapore	231	176	-23.8	Netherlands	1,676	1,792	6.9
Thailand	836	794	-5.0	Norway	244	270	10.7
Vietnam	218	286	31.2	Portugal	115	143	24.3
				Spain	17,176	18,865	9.8
EUROPE	**100,668**	**109,907**	**9.2**	Sweden	598	818	36.8
Europe, Unspecified	214	0	-100.0	Switzerland	1,022	1,148	12.3
				United Kingdom	30,143	31,706	5.2
Eastern Europe	**4,150**	**5,017**	**20.9**	Vatican City	30	0	-100.0
Albania	0	6	0.0	Western Europe, Unspec.	20	0	-100.0

22 (cont'd) HOST REGIONS AND DESTINATIONS OF U.S. STUDY ABROAD STUDENTS, 2001/02 & 2002/03

Destination	2001/02	2002/03	% Change	Destination	2001/02	2002/03	% Change
LATIN AMERICA	**23,300**	**26,643**	**14.3**	Paraguay	16	59	268.8
Latin America, Unspec.	12	0	-100.0	Peru	522	599	14.8
				Suriname	0	0	-
Caribbean	**3,498**	**4,075**	**16.5**	Uruguay	52	59	13.5
Anguilla	7	13	85.7	Venezuela	97	57	-41.2
Aruba	1	11	1,000.0	S. America, Unspecified	1	0	-100.0
Antigua	0	0	-				
Bahamas	414	535	29.2	**MIDDLE EAST**	**1,310**	**648**	**-50.5**
Barbados	126	162	28.6	Bahrain	3	0	-100.0
British Virgin Islands	55	119	116.4	Cyprus	77	10	-87.0
Cayman Islands	35	43	22.9	Iran	2	1	-50.0
Cuba	1,279	1,474	15.2	Israel	1,031	340	-67.0
Dominica	35	0	-100.0	Jordan	37	29	-21.6
Dominican Republic	596	651	9.2	Kuwait	4	6	50.0
Grenada	9	0	-100.0	Lebanon	16	14	-12.5
Guadeloupe	49	22	-55.1	Oman	1	0	-100.0
Haiti	105	92	-12.4	Palestinian Authority	0	0	-
Jamaica	405	539	33.1	Saudi Arabia	1	2	100.0
Martinique	82	73	-11.0	Syria	2	4	100.0
Montserrat	5	0	-100.0	Turkey	129	228	76.7
Netherlands Antilles	20	13	-35.0	United Arab Emirates	7	12	71.4
St. Kitts-Nevis	7	12	71.4	Yemen	0	1	-
St. Lucia	0	0	-	Middle East, Unspecified	0	1	-
St. Vincent	0	6	-				
Trinidad & Tobago	175	107	-38.9	**NORTH AMERICA**	**1,251**	**1,251**	**0.0**
Turks & Caicos Islands	10	19	90.0	Bermuda	71	57	-19.7
Windward Islands	1	0	-100.0	Canada	1,180	1,194	1.2
Caribbean, Unspecified	82	184	124.4				
				ANTARCTICA	**0**	**18**	**-**
Central America/Mexico	**14,023**	**15,859**	**13.1**				
Belize	681	1,363	100.1	**OCEANIA**	**10,952**	**12,749**	**16.4**
Costa Rica	3,781	4,296	13.6	Australia	9,456	10,691	13.1
El Salvador	145	117	-19.3	Cook Islands	3	1	-66.7
Guatemala	410	446	8.8	Fed. States of Micronesia	22	16	-27.3
Honduras	332	462	39.2	Fiji	45	66	46.7
Mexico	8,078	8,775	8.6	French Polynesia	40	7	-82.5
Nicaragua	251	290	15.5	Marshall Islands	2	8	300.0
Panama	344	109	-68.3	New Zealand	1,326	1,917	44.6
C. America/Mexico, Unspec.	1	1	0.0	Palau	7	0	-100.0
				Papua New Guinea	4	0	-100.0
South America	**5,767**	**6,709**	**16.3**	Tonga	10	0	-100.0
Argentina	905	868	-4.1	Vanuatu	0	4	-
Bolivia	156	159	1.9	Western Samoa	26	25	-3.8
Brazil	1,064	1,345	26.4	Pacific Islands, Unspec.	11	14	27.3
Chile	1,492	1,944	30.3				
Colombia	26	15	-42.3	**MULTI-COUNTRY**	**7,899**	**8,835**	**11.8**
Ecuador	1,425	1,567	10.0				
French Guiana	2	0	-100.0	**TOTAL**	**160,920**	**174,629**	**8.5**
Guyana	9	37	311.1				

22 (cont'd) HOST REGIONS AND DESTINATIONS OF U.S. STUDY ABROAD STUDENTS, 2001/02 & 2002/03

PERCENT OF U.S. STUDY ABROAD STUDENTS

Field of Study	1993/94	1994/95	1995/96	1996/97	1997/98*	1998/99	1999/00	2000/01	2001/02	2002/03
Social Sciences	-	-	-	-	-	20.3	20.1	20.3	21.9	21.3
Business & Management	13.6	13.5	13.9	14.6	15.6	17.7	17.7	18.1	17.6	17.7
Humanities	-	-	-	-	-	14.6	14.5	14.5	13.8	13.3
Fine or Applied Arts	7.7	9.0	6.8	7.1	7.7	8.0	8.6	8.5	8.5	9.0
Foreign Languages	11.3	10.3	10.7	9.3	8.0	8.1	8.2	8.2	8.5	7.9
Physical Sciences	5.3	6.8	6.8	6.8	7.0	7.4	7.4	7.1	7.6	7.1
Other	7.7	6.4	7.5	7.8	4.8	5.6	5.1	4.9	5.2	6.4
Education	4.0	3.8	3.7	4.3	4.5	4.2	4.2	4.4	3.9	4.1
Undeclared	3.6	3.3	3.9	3.9	4.2	4.3	5.1	4.5	3.8	3.5
Health Sciences	1.7	2.1	2.3	2.7	3.2	3.8	2.8	3.2	3.0	3.1
Engineering	2.3	2.2	2.1	1.9	2.7	2.8	2.9	2.7	2.9	2.9
Math & Computer Sciences	1.1	1.2	1.3	1.6	1.6	1.8	2.0	2.0	2.2	2.4
Agriculture	0.9	0.7	1.0	1.2	1.5	1.4	1.4	1.6	1.1	1.5
Social Sciences & Humanities	37.1	36.6	35.2	34.0	34.8	-	-	-	-	-
Dual Major	3.6	4.1	4.7	4.9	4.3	-	-	-	-	-
Total	**76,302**	**84,403**	**89,242**	**99,448**	**113,959**	**129,770**	**143,590**	**154,168**	**160,920**	**174,629**

*Social Sciences & Humanities were combined until 1998/99.

23   FIELDS OF STUDY OF U.S. STUDY ABROAD STUDENTS, 1993/94 – 2002/03

PERCENT OF U.S. STUDY ABROAD STUDENTS

Duration	1993/94	1994/95	1995/96	1996/97	1997/98	1998/99	1999/00	2000/01	2001/02	2002/03
One Semester	37.2	39.4	39.4	40.2	38.4	39.8	38.1	38.5	39.0	40.3
Summer Term	30.9	30.0	31.4	32.8	33.8	34.6	34.2	33.7	34.4	32.7
Fewer Than 8 Weeks	1.7	2.5	3.5	3.3	4.2	4.8	7.3	7.4	7.3	9.4
Academic Year	14.3	14.0	12.1	10.7	9.5	8.6	8.2	7.3	7.8	6.7
January Term	5.6	6.9	5.6	6.8	6.6	6.5	6.0	7.0	6.0	5.6
One Quarter	6.3	4.8	5.1	4.0	4.8	4.0	4.7	4.1	3.9	3.8
Other	1.4	0.9	1.3	1.2	1.0	0.8	0.4	0.9	0.6	0.6
Calendar Year	0.5	0.5	0.7	0.2	0.5	0.2	0.4	0.6	0.5	0.5
Two Quarters	2.0	1.1	0.9	0.9	1.1	0.6	0.7	0.6	0.5	0.4
Total	**76,302**	**84,403**	**89,242**	**99,448**	**113,959**	**129,770**	**143,590**	**154,168**	**160,920**	**174,629**

24   DURATION OF U.S. STUDY ABROAD, 1993/94 – 2002/03

PERCENT OF U.S. STUDY ABROAD STUDENTS

	1993/94	1994/95	1995/96	1996/97	1997/98	1998/99	1999/00	2000/01	2001/02	2002/03
Academic level										
Junior	40.6	43.0	41.6	41.3	42.2	40.3	39.8	38.9	40.7	38.0
Senior	15.6	16.3	16.2	18.3	17.7	19.0	17.7	20.0	20.4	20.2
Bachelor's, Unspecified	19.1	17.5	18.1	14.7	13.2	13.3	15.6	13.5	11.0	15.3
Sophomore	11.8	10.8	12.1	12.8	13.4	13.2	13.6	14.0	13.6	11.8
Master's	4.0	4.1	3.7	4.2	5.1	4.5	5.0	4.5	4.7	4.8
Graduate, Unspecified	2.3	2.6	3.2	3.3	2.6	3.2	2.7	3.1	3.3	3.4
Freshman	3.5	2.5	2.0	2.4	2.7	2.5	3.2	3.1	3.2	2.9
Associate's	1.6	1.3	2.0	1.9	2.3	2.5	0.9	0.9	1.5	2.1
Doctoral	0.7	0.5	0.4	0.3	0.4	0.5	0.6	0.7	0.7	0.9
Other	0.8	1.5	0.7	0.8	0.5	1.1	1.0	1.1	0.8	0.7
Sex										
Female	62.9	62.2	65.3	64.9	64.8	65.2	64.6	65.0	64.9	64.7
Male	37.1	37.8	34.7	35.1	35.2	34.8	35.4	35.0	35.1	35.3
Race/Ethnicity										
Caucasian	83.8	86.4	84.4	83.9	84.5	85.0	83.7	84.3	82.9	83.2
Asian-American	5.0	4.9	5.1	5.0	4.8	4.4	4.8	5.4	5.8	6.0
Hispanic-American	5.0	4.5	5.0	5.1	5.5	5.2	5.0	5.4	5.4	5.1
African-American	2.8	2.8	2.9	3.5	3.8	3.3	3.5	3.5	3.5	3.4
Multiracial	3.1	1.1	2.3	2.1	0.8	1.2	0.9	0.9	2	1.8
Native American	0.3	0.3	0.3	0.3	0.6	0.9	0.5	0.5	0.4	0.5
Visa Students	-	-	-	-	-	-	1.6	-	-	-
Total	**76,302**	**84,403**	**89,242**	**99,448**	**113,959**	**129,770**	**143,590**	**154,168**	**160,920**	**174,629**

* Separate data on visa students were collected in 1999/00.

25   PROFILE OF U.S. STUDY ABROAD STUDENTS, 1993/94 – 2002/03

Carnegie Category	1999/00 %	2000/01 %	2001/02 %	2002/03 %	2002/03 Avg. # of Institutions
Doctoral/Research Extensive & Intensive	57.9	57.9	58.6	60.1	462
Master's I & II	19.8	20.5	20.5	20.5	106
Baccalaureate	18.5	18.0	17.6	16.6	103
Associate's	2.3	2.4	2.2	2.1	26
Specialized	1.4	1.2	1.0	0.8	17
Total	**143,590**	**154,168**	**160,920**	**174,629**	

For-Credit Internships or Work Abroad by Carnegie Type	1999/00 %	1999/00 # of Institutions	2000/01 %	2000/01 # of Institutions	2001/02 %	2001/02 # of Institutions	2002/03 %	2002/03 # of Institutions
Doctoral/Research Extensive & Intensive	56.8	85	51.1	85	56.7	107	52.1	100
Master's I & II	17.3	101	21.8	110	17.0	112	24.1	103
Baccalaureate	22.4	86	24.4	86	19.1	86	19.3	98
Associate's	1.3	6	0.5	5	1.9	7	2.3	11
Specialized	2.2	7	2.3	10	5.3	8	2.1	9
Students/Total Institutions	**5,584**	**285**	**6,950**	**296**	**7,331**	**320**	**8,477**	**321**

Program Sponsorship	1993/94 %	1994/95 %	1995/96 %	1996/97 %	1997/98 %	1998/99 %	1999/00 %	2000/01 %	2001/02 %	2002/03 %
Solely Own Institution	73.4	71.2	71.9	72.9	74.1	73.9	73.9	72.3	73.1	71.6
Other Institutions/Organizations	26.6	28.8	28.1	27.1	25.9	26.1	26.1	27.7	26.9	28.3
Total	**76,302**	**84,403**	**89,242**	**99,448**	**113,959**	**129,770**	**143,590**	**154,168**	**160,920**	**174,629**

Financial Support	2002/03 (%) Institution's Own Programs	2002/03 (%) Institution-Sponsored	2002/03 (%) Other Programs
Federal Aid	72.0	68.4	25.5
State Aid	67.4	61.9	19.2
Need-Based Institutional Aid	65.1	53.1	11.6
Merit-Based Institutional Aid	65.3	50.4	11.7
Other Aid	53.5	46.4	13.9
Number of Responding Institutions	**771**	**721**	**616**

26 HOME INSTITUTIONAL TYPE, FOR-CREDIT INTERNSHIPS, OR WORK ABROAD, 1999/00 – 2002/03; PROGRAM SPONSORSHIP, 1993/94 – 2002/03; AND FINANCIAL SUPPORT FOR U.S. STUDY ABROAD STUDENTS, 2002/03

Rank	Institution	City	State	Study Abroad Students	Undergraduate Study Abroad Students	Total UG Degrees Conferred IPEDS 2002	Estimated % UG Participation In Study Abroad
1	Wake Forest University	Winston-Salem	NC	524	524	906	57.8
2	Georgetown University	Washington	DC	1,290	922	1,666	55.3
3	Dartmouth College	Hanover	NH	599	599	1,101	54.4
3	University of St. Thomas	St. Paul	MN	649	584	1,073	54.4
5	Pepperdine University	Malibu	CA	574	459	858	53.5
6	University of Notre Dame	Notre Dame	IN	1,181	999	1,985	50.3
7	University of Denver	Denver	CO	521	377	758	49.7
8	Worcester Polytechnic Institute	Worcester	MA	304	304	614	49.5
9	Duke University	Durham	NC	868	738	1,579	46.7
10	Tufts University	Medford	MA	563	537	1,246	43.1
11	George Washington University	Washington	DC	865	757	1,826	41.5
12	American University	Washington	DC	652	506	1,226	41.3
13	Syracuse University	Syracuse	NY	1,116	1,007	2,582	39.0
14	Emory University	Atlanta	GA	778	671	1,776	37.8
15	New York University	New York	NY	2,061	1,792	4,786	37.4
16	Vanderbilt University	Nashville	TN	513	492	1,393	35.3
17	Cornell University	Ithaca	NY	1,077	763	2,187	34.9
18	U. of North Carolina at Chapel Hill	Chapel Hill	NC	1,426	1,233	3,560	34.6
19	Boston College	Chestnut Hill	MA	851	772	2,311	33.4
20	Tulane University	New Orleans	LA	843	444	1,356	32.7

27A INSTITUTIONS BY ESTIMATED UNDERGRADUATE PARTICIPATION IN STUDY ABROAD: TOP 20 DOCTORAL/RESEARCH INSTITUTIONS, 2002/03

Rank	Institution	City	State	Study Abroad Students
1	New York University	New York	NY	2,061
2	University of California – Los Angeles	Los Angeles	CA	1,917
3	Michigan State University	East Lansing	MI	1,864
4	University of Texas at Austin	Austin	TX	1,654
5	University of Arizona	Tucson	AZ	1,466
6	University of Wisconsin – Madison	Madison	WI	1,441
7	University of North Carolina at Chapel Hill	Chapel Hill	NC	1,426
8	University of Georgia	Athens	GA	1,401
9	Indiana University at Bloomington	Bloomington	IN	1,379
10	University of Illinois at Urbana-Champaign	Urbana	IL	1,377
11	Boston University	Boston	MA	1,369
12	University of Florida	Gainesville	FL	1,357
13	Penn State University – University Park	University Park	PA	1,351
14	University of Minnesota – Twin Cities	Minneapolis	MN	1,294
15	Georgetown University	Washington	DC	1,290
16	Arizona State University – Tempe Campus	Tempe	AZ	1,278

27B INSTITUTIONS BY TOTAL NUMBER OF STUDY ABROAD STUDENTS: TOP 20 DOCTORAL/RESEARCH INSTITUTIONS, 2002/03

Rank	Institution	City	State	Study Abroad Students
17	University of Pennsylvania	Philadelphia	PA	1,228
18	The Ohio State University, Main Campus	Columbus	OH	1,227
19	Miami University – Oxford	Oxford	OH	1,208
20	University of Southern California	Los Angeles	CA	1,207

**27B   (cont'd) INSTITUTIONS BY TOTAL NUMBER OF STUDY ABROAD STUDENTS:
TOP 20 DOCTORAL/RESEARCH INSTITUTIONS, 2002/03**

Rank	Institution	City	State	Study Abroad Students	Undergraduate Study Abroad Students	Total UG Degrees Conferred IPEDS 2002	Estimated % UG Participation In Study Abroad
1	Lynn University	Boca Raton	FL	800	707	335	211.0
2	Elon University	Elon	NC	737	729	842	86.6
3	Queens University of Charlotte	Charlotte	NC	141	141	219	64.4
4	Warren Wilson College	Ashville	NC	100	100	167	59.9
5	Gonzaga University	Spokane	WA	311	311	571	54.5
6	Loyola College in Maryland	Baltimore	MD	410	410	785	52.2
7	Whitworth College	Spokane	WA	196	191	372	51.3
8	Hamline University	St. Paul	MN	201	201	419	48.0
9	University of Richmond	Richmond	VA	384	320	753	42.5
10	Bethel College	St. Paul	MN	275	270	646	41.8
11	University of Redlands	Redlands	CA	310	303	728	41.6
12	University of Portland	Portland	OR	216	211	543	38.9
13	Centenary College of Louisiana	Shreveport	LA	81	81	209	38.8
13	Samford University	Birmingham	AL	262	227	585	38.8
15	Pacific Lutheran University	Tacoma	WA	290	290	763	38.0
15	William Carey College	Hattiesburg	MS	150	148	389	38.0
17	Marygrove College	Detroit	MI	43	43	116	37.1
18	University of St. Thomas	Houston	TX	120	110	298	36.9
19	Arcadia University	Glenside	PA	144	131	359	36.5
20	University of Tampa	Tampa	FL	197	197	558	35.3

**28A   INSTITUTIONS BY ESTIMATED UNDERGRADUATE PARTICIPATION IN STUDY ABROAD:
TOP 20 MASTER'S INSTITUTIONS, 2002/03**

Rank	Institution	City	State	Study Abroad Students
1	Lynn University	Boca Raton	FL	800
2	Elon University	Elon	NC	737
3	James Madison University	Harrisonburg	VA	626
4	California Polytechnic State U. – San Luis Obispo	San Luis Obispo	CA	549
5	Villanova University	Villanova	PA	534
6	Truman State University	Kirksville	MO	495
7	Appalachian State University	Boone	NC	438
8	University of Northern Iowa	Cedar Falls	IA	413
9	Loyola College in Maryland	Baltimore	MD	410
10	Johnson & Wales University	Providence	RI	389
11	University of Richmond	Richmond	VA	384
12	Bentley College	Waltham	MA	372
13	College of Charleston	Charleston	SC	371
14	Ithaca College	Ithaca	NY	365
15	Grand Valley State University	Allendale	MI	359
16	University of Wisconsin – Stevens Point	Stevens Point	WI	357
17	St. Cloud State University	St. Cloud	MN	351
18	University of Wisconsin – Eau Claire	Eau Claire	WI	332
19	University of Minnesota – Duluth	Duluth	MN	317
20	Texas State University – San Marcos	San Marcos	TX	312

28B INSTITUTIONS BY TOTAL NUMBER OF STUDY ABROAD STUDENTS: TOP 20 MASTER'S INSTITUTIONS, 2002/03

Rank	Institution	City	State	Study Abroad Students	Undergraduate Study Abroad Students	Total UG Degrees Conferred IPEDS 2002	Estimated % UG Participation In Study Abroad
1	Austin College	Sherman	TX	376	375	306	122.5
2	DePauw University	Greencastle	IN	468	458	472	97.0
3	Dickinson College	Carlisle	PA	433	433	457	94.7
4	Eckerd College	St. Petersburg	FL	318	318	339	93.8
5	St. Olaf College	Northfield	MN	641	641	692	92.6
6	Centre College	Danville	KY	214	214	255	83.9
7	Colby College	Waterville	ME	386	386	471	82.0
8	Lyon College	Batesville	AR	63	63	79	79.7
9	Linfield College	McMinnville	OR	250	250	320	78.1
10	Principia College	Elsah	IL	98	94	124	75.8
11	Earlham College	Richmond	IN	195	195	263	74.1
12	Davidson College	Davidson	NC	320	320	434	73.7
13	Colorado College	Colorado Springs	CO	392	392	534	73.4
14	Pitzer College	Claremont	CA	127	127	177	71.8
15	Bates College	Lewiston	ME	310	299	417	71.7
16	Wingate University	Wingate	NC	138	138	195	70.8
17	Carleton College	Northfield	MN	345	345	494	69.8
18	Hartwick College	Oneonta	NY	198	198	287	69.0
19	Concordia College – Moorhead	Moorhead	MN	413	413	607	68.0
19	Luther College	Decorah	IA	389	389	572	68.0

**29A   INSTITUTIONS BY ESTIMATED UNDERGRADUATE PARTICIPATION IN STUDY ABROAD:
TOP 20 BACCALAUREATE INSTITUTIONS, 2002/03**

Rank	Institution	City	State	Study Abroad Students
1	St. Olaf College	Northfield	MN	641
2	Calvin College	Grand Rapids	MI	524
3	DePauw University	Greencastle	IN	468
4	Dickinson College	Carlisle	PA	433
5	Concordia College – Moorhead	Moorhead	MN	413
6	Middlebury College	Middlebury	VT	411
7	Messiah College	Grantham	PA	398
8	Gustavus Adolphus College	St. Peter	MN	395
9	Colorado College	Colorado Springs	CO	392
10	Luther College	Decorah	IA	389
11	Colby College	Waterville	ME	386
12	Bucknell University	Lewisburg	PA	383
13	Union College	Schenectady	NY	382
14	Austin College	Sherman	TX	376
15	Wellesley College	Wellesley	MA	374
16	Lafayette College	Easton	PA	370
17	Smith College	Northampton	MA	365
18	Carleton College	Northfield	MN	345
19	Davidson College	Davidson	NC	320
20	Eckerd College	St. Petersburg	FL	318

29B INSTITUTIONS BY TOTAL NUMBER OF STUDY ABROAD STUDENTS: TOP 20 BACCALAUREATE INSTITUTIONS, 2002/03

INTENSIVE ENGLISH

% of Students Intending Further Study	# of Programs	Average # of Students Per Program	Total Students All Programs	Average # of Student-Weeks Per Program	Total Student-Weeks All Programs
30% and Less	40	451	18,022	4,869	194,759
31% to 60%	37	207	7,660	2,522	93,299
61% and Greater	54	167	9,027	2,333	125,957
All Reporting Programs*	131	265	34,709	3,160	41,4015
All Programs	181		43,303		495,939

* 50 programs did not provide further study data.

30   IEP STUDENTS AND STUDENT-WEEKS BY THE PERCENTAGE OF STUDENTS INTENDING TO CONTINUE FURTHER (NON-IEP) STUDY IN THE U.S., 2003

Rank	Place of Origin	2001 Total Students	2002 Total Students	2003 Total Students	% Change 2001-2003	2001 Student-Weeks	2002 Student-Weeks	2003 Student-Weeks	% Change 2001-2003
	WORLD TOTAL	78,521	51,179	43,003	-45.2	865,603	565,174	495,939	-42.7
1	Japan	16,470	13,047	10,519	-36.1	187,500	145,602	122,084	-34.9
2	Korea, Republic of	13,110	10,000	10,412	-20.6	175,218	129,341	132,965	-24.1
3	Taiwan	7,605	5,919	4,235	-44.3	77,718	64,114	52,707	-32.2
4	Italy	1,924	1,171	1,408	-26.8	11,296	8,096	8,034	-28.9
5	Brazil	5,253	2,363	1,359	-74.1	41,254	18,121	11,782	-71.4
6	France	1,587	1,231	1,156	-27.2	12,662	8,530	10,231	-19.2
7	Turkey	2,254	1,102	1,034	-54.1	24,264	11,224	12,408	-48.9
8	Thailand	1,929	1,245	943	-51.1	24,642	15,630	12,899	-47.7
9	Mexico	4,369	936	883	-79.8	43,907	10,998	8,942	-79.6
10	Colombia	2,255	1,089	858	-62.0	27,132	13,309	10,850	-60.0
11	Germany	1,396	1,199	849	-39.2	13,326	8,885	7,266	-45.5
12	China	1,760	1,048	796	-54.8	22,052	13,517	9,276	-57.9
13	Venezuela	2,487	1,216	742	-70.2	27,346	14,637	8,800	-67.8
14	Switzerland	1,584	1,564	732	-53.8	13,529	12,380	6,577	-51.4
15	Spain	742	539	728	-1.9	6,401	5,142	6,200	-3.1
16	Saudi Arabia	2,191	756	348	-84.1	29,674	11,997	5,466	-81.6
17	Chile	664	330	344	-48.2	5,157	2,489	3,076	-40.4
18	Ecuador	449	234	298	-33.6	4,571	2,550	3,699	-19.1
19	Russia	400	292	273	-31.8	4,353	3,103	2,894	-33.5
20	Peru	475	298	269	-43.4	5,773	3,700	3,218	-44.3

31   LEADING PLACES OF ORIGIN OF IEP STUDENTS, 2001 – 2003

Place of Origin	2003 Students	2003 Student-Weeks
AFRICA	**806**	**10,593**
East Africa	**65**	**740**
Burundi	1	9
Comoros	4	20
Eritrea	1	17
Ethiopia	18	216
Kenya	13	170
Madagascar	1	15
Malawi	0	0
Mauritius	1	7
Mozambique	3	24
Rwanda	4	45
Somalia	6	37
Tanzania	12	167
Uganda	1	13
Zambia	0	0
Zimbabwe	0	0
Central Africa	**178**	**2,607**
Angola	19	301
Cameroon	50	602
Central African Republic	3	41
Chad	8	66
Congo	29	531
Congo/Zaire	2	28
Equatorial Guinea	1	8
Gabon	66	1,030
São Tomé & Príncipe	0	0
North Africa	**176**	**1,743**
Algeria	28	303
Egypt	36	296
Libya	8	137
Morocco	85	786
Sudan	8	81
Tunisia	11	140
Southern Africa	**3**	**37**
Botswana	0	0
Namibia	0	0
South Africa	3	37
Swaziland	0	0

Place of Origin	2003 Students	2003 Student-Weeks
West Africa	**384**	**5,466**
Benin	6	78
Burkina Faso	30	444
Côte d'Ivoire	65	902
Gambia	2	8
Ghana	15	179
Guinea	47	717
Guinea-Bissau	1	11
Liberia	3	60
Mali	74	1,049
Mauritania	15	314
Niger	28	381
Nigeria	18	245
Senegal	52	711
Sierra Leone	0	0
Togo	28	367
ASIA	**28,026**	**344,927**
East Asia	**26,275**	**321,556**
China	796	9,275
Hong Kong	130	1,711
Japan	10,519	122,082
Korea, Dem. People's Rep.	25	774
Korea, Republic of	10,412	132,963
Macao	4	91
Mongolia	154	1,953
Taiwan	4,235	52,707
South/Central Asia	**309**	**3,944**
Afghanistan	7	50
Bangladesh	11	165
Bhutan	0	0
India	101	1,017
Kazakhstan	57	895
Kyrgyzstan	8	153
Nepal	28	342
Pakistan	20	242
Sri Lanka	10	153
Tajikistan	9	115
Turkmenistan	9	91
Uzbekistan	49	721
Southeast Asia	**1,442**	**19,427**
Brunei	0	0

Place of Origin	2003 Students	2003 Student-Weeks	Place of Origin	2003 Students	2003 Student-Weeks
Cambodia	23	362	Moldova	3	49
Indonesia	153	1,905	Poland	214	2,272
Laos	6	80	Romania	15	225
Malaysia	31	422	Russia	273	2,894
Myanmar	17	310	Slovakia	25	339
Philippines	22	547	Slovenia	7	28
Singapore	2	45	Ukraine	73	929
Thailand	943	12,899	Yugoslavia, Former	37	439
Vietnam	245	2,857			
			Western Europe	**5,688**	**45,313**
MIDDLE EAST	**1,845**	**23,758**	Austria	216	1,454
Bahrain	7	79	Belgium	186	1,851
Cyprus	21	118	Denmark	56	443
Iran	59	700	Finland	31	181
Iraq	5	31	France	1,156	10,231
Israel	44	464	Germany	849	7,266
Jordan	26	351	Greece	18	220
Kuwait	106	1,472	Iceland	2	34
Lebanon	17	181	Ireland	0	0
Oman	7	109	Italy	1,408	8,034
Palestinian Authority	19	223	Liechtenstein	2	17
Qatar	12	187	Luxembourg	0	0
Saudi Arabia	348	5,465	Netherlands	108	1,036
Syria	30	367	Norway	40	439
Turkey	1,034	12,407	Portugal	43	263
United Arab Emirates	103	1,522	San Marino	0	0
Yemen	7	82	Spain	728	6,200
			Sweden	108	1,025
EUROPE	**6,703**	**56,675**	Switzerland	732	6,577
			United Kingdom	5	42
Eastern Europe	**1,015**	**11,362**	Vatican City	0	0
Albania	17	220			
Armenia	10	140	**LATIN AMERICA**	**5,590**	**59,676**
Azerbaijan	16	211			
Belarus	17	245	**Caribbean**	**126**	**1,463**
Bosnia & Herzegovina	13	132	Aruba	0	0
Bulgaria	64	862	Antigua	2	4
Croatia	24	138	Bahamas	2	8
Czech Republic	87	779	British Virgin Islands	0	0
Estonia	3	21	Cuba	13	170
Georgia	18	177	Dominican Republic	65	688
Hungary	62	792	Guadeloupe	3	37
Latvia	10	122	Haiti	37	540
Lithuania	21	280	Jamaica	3	1
Macedonia	6	68	Martinique	0	0

32 (cont'd) REGIONS AND PLACES OF ORIGIN OF IEP STUDENTS, 2003

Place of Origin	2003 Students	2003 Student-Weeks	Place of Origin	2003 Students	2003 Student-Weeks
Montserrat	0	0	Paraguay	38	376
Netherlands Antilles	1	15	Peru	269	3,218
St. Lucia	0	0	Suriname	0	0
			Uruguay	33	359
Central America/Mexico	**1,183**	**12,577**	Venezuela	742	8,800
Belize	0	0			
Costa Rica	40	400	**NORTH AMERICA**	**27**	**253**
El Salvador	44	586	Canada	27	253
Guatemala	46	507			
Honduras	30	524	**OCEANIA**	**5**	**42**
Mexico	883	8,942	Australia	0	0
Nicaragua	28	365	Fiji	0	0
Panama	112	1,253	French Polynesia	4	17
			Kiribati	0	0
South America	**4,281**	**45,636**	New Caledonia	0	0
Argentina	257	2,364	New Zealand	1	25
Bolivia	81	1,108	Tonga	0	0
Brazil	1,359	11,782	Western Samoa	0	0
Chile	344	3,076			
Colombia	858	10,850	**STATELESS**	**1**	**15**
Ecuador	298	3,699			
Falkland Islands	2	4	**WORLD TOTAL**	**43,003**	**495,939**

32 (cont'd) REGIONS AND PLACES OF ORIGIN OF IEP STUDENTS, 2003

State	Reporting Programs	Total Students	Total Student-Weeks
Alabama	1	208	3,174
Arkansas	3	246	3,686
California	25	13,246	138,874
Colorado	6	736	10,008
Connecticut	1	111	1,341
District of Columbia	3	860	6,953
Delaware	1	594	4,524
Florida	12	2,677	23,257
Georgia	3	1,338	13,349
Guam	1	0	0
Hawaii	2	538	10,842
Idaho	1	0	0
Iowa	1	118	1,913
Illinois	3	626	6,772
Indiana	5	897	12,518
Kansas	2	214	3,255
Kentucky	2	0	0
Louisiana	1	87	1,064
Massachussetts	5	2,536	21,092
Maryland	1	152	2,204
Maine	1	21	318
Michigan	3	238	2,944
Minnesota	2	312	3,730
Missouri	3	231	4,184
North Carolina	3	562	4,228
North Dakota	1	0	0
Nebraska	1	277	4,741
New Mexico	1	38	679
New Jersey	2	302	3,687
New York	18	4,255	46,492
Ohio	5	566	8,206
Oklahoma	5	731	9,161
Oregon	7	994	12,687
Pennsylvania	9	2,139	27,999
South Carolina	2	242	2,616
Tennessee	5	475	7,379
Texas	12	1,943	26,027
Utah	3	706	14,898
Virginia	4	495	5,348
Washington	9	2,692	38,223
Wisconsin	3	498	5,823
West Virginia	1	96	1,718
Wyoming	2	6	25
U.S. TOTAL	**181**	**43,003**	**495,939**

33   IEP STUDENTS BY STATE, 2003

CALIFORNIA		NEW YORK	
	% of Students		% of Students
Part-Time	14.7	Part-Time	16.8
Full-Time	85.3	Full-Time	83.2
State Totals	13,246	State Totals	4,255
	% Student-Weeks		% Student-Weeks
Part-Time	7.1	Part-Time	12.6
Full-Time	92.9	Full-Time	87.4
State Totals	138,874	State Totals	46,492

TEXAS		FLORIDA	
	% of Students		% of Students
Part-Time	29.4	Part-Time	24.2
Full-Time	70.6	Full-Time	75.8
State Totals	1,943	State Totals	2,677
	% Student-Weeks		% Student-Weeks
Part-Time	30.4	Part-Time	13.3
Full-Time	69.6	Full-Time	86.7
State Totals	26,027	State Totals	23,257

*Full-time enrollment is 18 class-hours a week or more; part-time study is less than 18 class-hours.

34 IEP STUDENTS AND STUDENT-WEEKS BY ENROLLMENT STATUS IN SELECTED LEADING STATES, 2003

CALIFORNIA

Rank	Place of Origin	Students	Student-Weeks	% of Students
1	Japan	3,673	35,223	27.7
2	Korea, Republic of	2,922	30,040	22.1
3	Taiwan	1,406	15,550	10.6
4	Italy	578	2,947	4.4
5	Switzerland	421	3,793	3.2
6	Germany	420	3,627	3.2
7	France	409	4,605	3.1
8	Brazil	370	2,696	2.8
9	Turkey	292	3,190	2.2
10	Spain	271	1,885	2.0
11	China	234	2,566	1.8
12	Thailand	232	2,991	1.8
13	Vietnam	113	1,339	0.9
14	Colombia	112	1,405	0.8
15	Austria	109	783	0.8
	State Totals	**13,246**	**138,874**	

NEW YORK

Rank	Place of Origin	Students	Student-Weeks	% of Students
1	Japan	1,195	16,232	28.1
2	Korea, Republic of	1,065	16,456	25.0
3	Taiwan	379	4,109	8.9
4	Turkey	157	2,486	3.7
5	Italy	129	1,025	3.0
6	France	110	967	2.6
7	Brazil	86	1,175	2.0
8	Thailand	83	1,224	2.0
9	China	81	921	1.9
10	Colombia	71	1,296	1.7
11	Germany	65	589	1.5
12	Spain	62	748	1.5
13	Mexico	47	415	1.1
14	Poland	42	614	1.0
15	Russia	40	560	0.9
	State Totals	**4,255**	**46,492**	

TEXAS

Rank	Place of Origin	Students	Student-Weeks	% of Students
1	Korea, Republic of	506	7,302	26.0
2	Taiwan	247	3,223	12.7
3	Japan	239	3,431	12.3
4	Mexico	126	1,430	6.5
5	China	94	1,016	4.8
6	Turkey	91	1,201	4.7
7	Venezuela	72	813	3.7
8	Brazil	56	565	2.9
9	Colombia	53	727	2.7
10	Thailand	49	636	2.5
11	India	26	349	1.3
12	Saudi Arabia	25	269	1.3
13	Russia	22	230	1.1
14	France	20	141	1.0
15	Italy	19	130	1.0
	State Totals	**1,943**	**26,027**	

FLORIDA

Rank	Place of Origin	Students	Student-Weeks	% of Students
1	Italy	330	1,310	12.3
2	Japan	325	3,001	12.1
3	France	233	1,521	8.7
4	Korea, Republic of	223	2,920	8.3
5	Venezuela	191	2,003	7.1
6	Brazil	156	1,064	5.8
7	Germany	137	931	5.1
8	Switzerland	123	954	4.6
9	Spain	101	505	3.8
10	Colombia	67	680	2.5
11	Taiwan	59	598	2.2
12	Turkey	49	424	1.8
13	Saudi Arabia	44	642	1.6
14	Austria	40	228	1.5
15	Belgium	35	212	1.3
	State Totals	**2,677**	**23,257**	

35   TOP 15 PLACES OF ORIGIN OF IEP STUDENTS IN SELECTED LEADING HOST STATES, 2003

Program Type/Membership	# of Programs	Total # of Students	Total Taking Less Than 18 Hours	Total Taking More Than 18 Hours	Total # of Student-Weeks	Student-Weeks Less Than 18 Hours	Student-Weeks More Than 18 Hours
Independent for-profit affiliated by contract with an institution of higher education	72	5,823	702	5,121	54,961	6,806	48,155
Independent for-profit not affiliated by contract with an institution of higher education	18	12,412	2,438	9,974	128,656	13,686	114,970
Independent not-for-profit affiliated by contract with an institution of higher education	3	1,634	100	1,534	19,685	264	19,421
Independent not-for-profit not affiliated by contract with an institution of higher education	2	396	15	381	4,922	147	4,775
Private college- or university-governed	27	5,465	1,413	4,052	81,879	20,594	61,285
Public college- or university-governed	59	17,273	2,104	15,169	205,836	26,420	179,416
Membership Affiliation							
AAIEP Only	128	25,189	4,527	20,662	293,513	40,107	253,406
UCIEP Only	2	414	56	358	6,389	808	5,581
Both AAIEP & UCIEP	30	12,823	1,724	11,099	157,049	22,069	134,980
Neither	21	4,577	465	4,112	38,988	4,933	34,055
All Programs	**181**	**43,003**	**6,772**	**36,231**	**495,939**	**67,917**	**428,022**

36   IEP STUDENTS AND STUDENT-WEEKS BY PROGRAM TYPE AND AFFILIATION, 2003

INTERNATIONAL SCHOLARS

Place of Origin	2002/03	2003/04	% Change		Place of Origin	2002/03	2003/04	% Change
AFRICA	**2,608**	**2,257**	**-13.5**		**West Africa**	**639**	**543**	**-15.0**
					Benin	9	14	55.6
East Africa	**629**	**544**	**-13.5**		Burkina Faso	13	14	7.7
Burundi	3	1	-66.7		Côte d'Ivoire	25	19	-24.0
Comoros	0	3	-		Gambia	11	10	-9.1
Eritrea	13	8	-38.5		Ghana	123	115	-6.5
Ethiopia	83	63	-24.1		Guinea	2	3	50.0
Kenya	229	197	-14.0		Liberia	14	6	-57.1
Madagascar	9	15	66.7		Mali	16	20	25.0
Malawi	8	9	12.5		Mauritania	5	4	-20.0
Mauritius	14	15	7.1		Niger	24	14	-41.7
Mozambique	5	6	20.0		Nigeria	330	259	-21.5
Rwanda	11	10	-9.1		Senegal	42	48	14.3
Somalia	3	4	33.3		Sierra Leone	20	9	-55.0
Tanzania	64	56	-12.5		Togo	5	8	60.0
Uganda	52	76	46.2					
Zambia	63	37	-41.3		**ASIA**	**39,119**	**39,121**	**0.0**
Zimbabwe	72	44	-38.9					
					East Asia	**29,690**	**29,382**	**-1.0**
Central Africa	**140**	**144**	**2.9**		China	15,206	14,871	-2.2
Angola	2	14	600.0		Hong Kong	174	182	4.6
Cameroon	82	62	-24.4		Japan	5,706	5,627	-1.4
Central African Republic	3	1	-66.7		Korea, Dem. People's Rep.	36	25	-30.6
Chad	30	32	6.7		Korea, Republic of	7,286	7,290	0.1
Congo	9	20	122.2		Macao	2	3	50.0
Congo/Zaire	6	5	-16.7		Mongolia	39	37	-5.1
Equatorial Guinea	2	4	100.0		Taiwan	1,241	1,347	8.5
Gabon	3	6	100.0					
São Tomé & Príncipe	3	0	-100.0		**South/Central Asia**	**7,852**	**8,086**	**3.0**
					Afghanistan	3	3	0.0
North Africa	**764**	**648**	**-15.2**		Bangladesh	289	240	-17.0
Algeria	101	63	-37.6		Bhutan	3	4	33.3
Canary Islands	2	0	-100.0		India	6,565	6,809	3.7
Egypt	448	374	-16.5		Kazakhstan	58	61	5.2
Libya	6	4	-33.3		Kyrgyzstan	47	49	4.3
Morocco	132	106	-19.7		Nepal	104	105	1.0
Sudan	22	19	-13.6		Pakistan	486	551	13.4
Tunisia	53	82	54.7		Republic of Maldives	0	1	0.0
					Sri Lanka	178	155	-12.9
Southern Africa	**436**	**378**	**-13.3**		Tajikistan	24	20	-16.7
Botswana	35	15	-57.1		Turkmenistan	13	8	-38.5
Lesotho	0	6	-		Uzbekistan	82	80	-2.4
Namibia	11	14	27.3					
South Africa	388	335	-13.7		**Southeast Asia**	**1,577**	**1,653**	**4.8**
Swaziland	2	8	300.0		Brunei	2	0	-100.0
					Cambodia	22	11	-50.0

37 INTERNATIONAL SCHOLAR TOTALS BY PLACE OF ORIGIN, 2002/03 & 2003/04

Place of Origin	2002/03	2003/04	% Change
Indonesia	284	208	-26.8
Laos	8	3	-62.5
Malaysia	170	176	3.5
Myanmar	19	18	-5.3
Philippines	303	318	5.0
Singapore	203	214	5.4
Thailand	442	572	29.4
Vietnam	124	133	7.3
EUROPE	**26,960**	**26,728**	**-0.9**
Eastern Europe	**7,260**	**6,603**	**-9.0**
Albania	49	57	16.3
Armenia	74	85	14.9
Azerbaijan	31	44	41.9
Belarus	104	81	-22.1
Bosnia & Herzegovina	47	23	-51.1
Bulgaria	270	308	14.1
Croatia	118	119	0.8
Czech Republic	374	316	-15.5
Estonia	44	38	-13.6
Georgia	121	106	-12.4
Hungary	493	399	-19.1
Latvia	57	39	-31.6
Lithuania	93	64	-31.2
Macedonia	39	38	-2.6
Moldova	53	59	11.3
Poland	872	927	6.3
Romania	622	575	-7.6
Russia	2,814	2,403	-14.6
Slovakia	143	169	18.2
Slovenia	58	40	-31.0
Ukraine	570	531	-6.8
Yugoslavia, Former	214	182	-15.0
Western Europe	**19,700**	**20,125**	**2.2**
Austria	429	347	-19.1
Belgium	365	395	8.2
Denmark	410	411	0.2
Finland	266	258	-3.0
France	2,789	2,842	1.9
Germany	4,648	4,737	1.9
Greece	528	537	1.7
Iceland	52	52	0.0
Ireland	311	360	15.8
Italy	2,242	2,317	3.3

Place of Origin	2002/03	2003/04	% Change
Liechtenstein	2	1	-50.0
Luxembourg	20	15	-25.0
Malta	0	9	-
Monaco	3	1	-66.7
Netherlands	955	975	2.1
Norway	333	307	-7.8
Portugal	239	246	2.9
San Marino	0	1	0.0
Spain	1,717	1,893	10.3
Sweden	662	642	-3.0
Switzerland	616	662	7.5
United Kingdom	3,113	3,117	0.1
LATIN AMERICA	**6,154**	**5,401**	**-12.2**
Caribbean	**664**	**335**	**-49.5**
Antigua	5	4	-20.0
Aruba	3	30	900.0
Bahamas	36	34	-5.6
Barbados	16	24	50.0
British Virgin Islands	3	3	0.0
Cuba	33	16	-51.5
Dominica	3	10	233.3
Dominican Republic	36	27	-25.0
Grenada	2	3	50.0
Guadeloupe	0	0	0.0
Haiti	19	19	0.0
Jamaica	168	69	-58.9
Martinique	0	0	-
Montserrat	2	1	-50.0
Netherlands Antilles	5	27	440.0
St. Kitts-Nevis	5	3	-40.0
St. Lucia	3	3	0.0
St. Vincent	2	3	50.0
Trinidad & Tobago	321	59	-81.6
Turks & Caicos Islands	2	0	-100.0
Central America/Mexico	**1,415**	**1,288**	**-9.0**
Belize	14	16	14.3
Costa Rica	75	69	-8.0
El Salvador	17	20	17.6
Guatemala	36	77	113.9
Honduras	35	30	-14.3
Mexico	1,185	1,032	-12.9
Nicaragua	6	9	50.0
Panama	47	35	-25.5

37 (cont'd) INTERNATIONAL SCHOLAR TOTALS BY PLACE OF ORIGIN, 2002/03 & 2003/04

Place of Origin	2002/03	2003/04	% Change		Place of Origin	2002/03	2003/04	% Change
South America	**4,075**	**3,778**	**-7.3**		Saudi Arabia	53	44	-17.0
Argentina	922	820	-11.1		Syria	93	106	14.0
Bolivia	33	38	15.2		Turkey	1,171	1,215	3.8
Brazil	1,458	1,341	-8.0		United Arab Emirates	8	21	162.5
Chile	258	291	12.8		Yemen	9	13	44.4
Colombia	525	524	-0.2					
Ecuador	99	82	-17.2		**NORTH AMERICA**	**4,228**	**4,128**	**-2.4**
Guyana	17	16	-5.9		Bermuda	6	3	-50.0
Paraguay	8	19	137.5		Canada	4,222	4,125	-2.3
Peru	269	207	-23.0					
Suriname	13	4	-69.2		**OCEANIA**	**1,547**	**1,521**	**-1.7**
Uruguay	74	101	36.5		Australia	1,183	1,197	1.2
Venezuela	399	335	-16.0		Fiji	0	5	-
					French Polynesia	0	1	0.0
MIDDLE EAST	**3,662**	**3,692**	**0.8**		Kiribati	0	0	-
Bahrain	11	25	127.3		New Zealand	360	317	-11.9
Cyprus	53	63	18.9		Niue	2	0	-
Iran	468	331	-29.3		Papua New Guinea	2	1	-50.0
Iraq	44	42	-4.5		Tonga	0	0	0.0
Israel	1,290	1,409	9.2					
Jordan	152	148	-2.6		**STATELESS**	**6**	**57**	**850.0**
Kuwait	25	30	20.0					
Lebanon	244	222	-9.0		**WORLD TOTAL**	**84,281**	**82,905**	**-1.6**
Oman	16	6	-62.5					
Palestinian Authority	20	16	-20.0					
Qatar	5	1	-80.0					

37 (cont'd) INTERNATIONAL SCHOLAR TOTALS BY PLACE OF ORIGIN, 2002/03 & 2003/04

Rank	Institution	City	State	2002/03	2003/04
1	Harvard University	Cambridge	MA	2,403	3,029
2	University of California – Los Angeles	Los Angeles	CA	2,098	2,130
3	University of California – Berkeley	Berkeley	CA	2,365	1,960
4	University of California – San Diego	La Jolla	CA	1,817	1,949
5	University of Pennsylvania	Philadelphia	PA	2,082	1,938
6	Columbia University	New York	NY	1,890	1,916
7	Yale University	New Haven	CT	1,637	1,770
8	University of Florida	Gainesville	FL	1,335	1,704
9	Stanford University	Stanford	CA	860	1,642
10	University of California – San Francisco	San Francisco	CA	1,600	1,600
11	Massachusetts Institute of Technology	Cambridge	MA	1,573	1,567
12	University of Washington	Seattle	WA	1,556	1,557
13	The Ohio State University, Main Campus	Columbus	OH	1,423	1,520
14	University of California – Irvine	Irvine	CA	597	1,478
15	University of Illinois at Urbana-Champaign	Champaign	IL	1,694	1,427
16	University of California – Davis	Davis	CA	1,109	1,356
17	University of Michigan – Ann Arbor	Ann Arbor	MI	1,342	1,291
18	University of Southern California	Los Angeles	CA	1,214	1,280
19	Cornell University	Ithaca	NY	1,236	1,242
20	University of Minnesota – Twin Cities	Minneapolis	MN	1,252	1,241
21	Washington University	St. Louis	MO	1,246	1,195
22	University of Wisconsin – Madison	Madison	WI	1,131	1,177
23	University of Illinois at Chicago	Chicago	IL	900	1,154
24	Duke University & Medical Center	Durham	NC	1,117	1,120
25	Boston University	Boston	MA	975	1,080
26	University of North Carolina at Chapel Hill	Chapel Hill	NC	1,024	1,047
27	University of Maryland College Park	College Park	MD	861	1,038
28	University of Iowa	Iowa City	IA	865	986
29	Michigan State University	East Lansing	MI	910	977
30	University of Texas at Austin	Austin	TX	1,013	946

38   LEADING INSTITUTIONS HOSTING INTERNATIONAL SCHOLARS, 2002/03 & 2003/04

State	1993/94 Total	1994/95 Total	1995/96 Total	1996/97 Total	1997/98 Total	1998/99 Total	1999/00 Total	2000/01 Total	2001/02 Total	2002/03 Total	2003/04 Total	% Change
Alabama	808	652	591	659	765	507	763	898	893	979	960	-1.9
Alaska	31	50	24	31	31	0*	0*	0*	0*	0*	0*	-
Arizona	688	515	835	887	889	1,095	1,199	1,191	1,168	1,308	1,121	-14.3
Arkansas	207	214	307	157	199	138	126	161	175	197	379	92.4
California	9,986	10,314	11,723	10,485	11,530	13,311	13,641	13,365	16,236	14,097	15,313	8.6
Colorado	1,062	1,156	922	946	920	1,109	1,122	1,272	1,376	1,412	1,400	-0.8
Connecticut	60	33	985	1,040	1,100	1,060	1,321	1,360	1,834	1,637	1,770	8.1
Delaware	793	328	363	366	327	374	677	386	455	455	421	-7.5
District of Columbia	330	731	779	742	544	741	776	648	610	511	525	2.7
Florida	1,633	1,820	1,661	1,822	1,858	1,770	2,114	2,436	2,552	2,427	2,987	23.1
Georgia	1,030	1,246	2,201	1,434	1,592	1,809	1,844	1,780	1,852	1,730	2,045	18.2
Hawaii	975	188	188	234	293	296	296	376	446	446	457	2.5
Idaho	54	46	321	272	76	64	103	113	136	167	141	-15.6
Illinois	2,340	2,374	1,741	2,847	2,892	3,379	3,545	4,048	4,392	4,144	2,849	-31.3
Indiana	1,700	1,438	1,550	1,672	1,754	1,600	1,994	1,826	1,950	2,036	1,735	-14.8
Iowa	830	774	922	1,139	941	1,260	1,276	1,500	1,441	1,511	1,105	-26.9
Kansas	595	362	313	413	343	423	425	581	451	423	651	53.9
Kentucky	305	368	445	482	517	580	412	600	635	387	580	49.9
Louisiana	444	539	505	486	591	567	851	626	713	743	746	0.4
Maine	47	63	54	28	34	81	75	116	159	110	107	-2.7
Maryland	912	668	737	1,117	1,647	1,059	1,417	1,506	1,965	1,970	1,444	-26.7
Massachusetts	5,807	5,185	5,274	5,044	5,219	5,184	5,181	6,180	6,340	5,858	6,798	16.0
Michigan	1,402	2,165	1,725	2,430	2,253	2,356	2,694	2,930	3,137	3,204	3,260	1.7
Minnesota	1,306	1,227	1,231	1,197	1,255	1,281	1,260	1,271	1,475	1,348	1,312	-2.7
Mississippi	255	178	171	164	161	232	302	285	347	229	364	59.0
Missouri	2,154	1,473	1,429	1,485	1,509	1,387	1,454	1,681	1,706	2,137	2,025	-5.2
Montana	73	93	113	128	112	132	133	248	234	129	225	74.4
Nebraska	281	300	244	357	207	538	312	537	599	594	655	10.3
Nevada	141	98	185	167	173	285	185	199	257	216	298	38.0
New Hampshire	188	195	240	234	324	355	443	468	437	440	494	12.3
New Jersey	1,006	919	520	472	558	630	564	1,209	1,195	1,223	1,516	24.0
New Mexico	200	210	222	168	257	239	237	304	340	260	439	68.8
New York	4,620	4,599	4,067	4,311	4,468	5,262	5,309	5,728	5,847	6,246	6,009	-3.8
North Carolina	1,511	1,424	1,463	1,414	1,776	1,684	1,968	2,145	2,581	2,929	2,944	0.5
North Dakota	174	53	57	98	87	85	91	139	129	230	256	11.3
Ohio	1,681	1,862	1,920	2,103	2,525	2,500	2,646	2,559	2,330	2,311	2,187	-5.4
Oklahoma	363	450	219	456	432	659	548	472	388	352	319	-9.4
Oregon	878	715	792	729	756	762	763	794	837	775	772	-0.4

State	1993/94 Total	1994/95 Total	1995/96 Total	1996/97 Total	1997/98 Total	1998/99 Total	1999/00 Total	2000/01 Total	2001/02 Total	2002/03 Total	2003/04 Total	% Change
Pennsylvania	3,594	3,681	3,277	4,012	3,858	4,357	4,557	4,655	5,463	5,517	5,020	-9.0
Rhode Island	281	341	399	449	434	408	383	528	528	425	0*	-
South Carolina	486	469	422	547	964	913	1,021	810	746	726	269	-62.9
South Dakota	19	10	23	35	14	21	8	18	17	8	8	0.0
Tennessee	1,105	1,197	1,000	1,087	893	1,055	1,169	1,751	1,663	1,676	869	-48.2
Texas	3,610	3,574	3,243	3,616	3,636	4,288	4,686	4,349	4,885	5,502	4,956	-9.9
Utah	338	448	383	505	511	558	567	669	492	393	389	-1.0
Vermont	228	207	200	189	209	203	228	231	0*	0*	0*	-
Virginia	1,030	1,015	1,017	1,042	1,191	1,427	1,423	1,553	1,438	1,227	1,128	-8.1
Washington	1,202	1,215	1,309	1,397	1,465	1,585	1,659	1,809	1,786	2,133	2,137	0.2
West Virginia	53	54	40	28	33	32	33	44	38	60	74	23.3
Wisconsin	1,044	750	888	1,077	1,243	730	652	1,191	1,247	1,281	1,261	-1.6
Wyoming	65	56	103	83	83	85	85	71	66	107	107	0.0
Puerto Rico	56	32	60	71	45	45	33	34	28	55	78	41.8
U.S. TOTAL	**59,981**	**58,074**	**59,403**	**62,354**	**65,494**	**70,501**	**74,571**	**79,651**	**86,015**	**84,281**	**82,905**	**-1.6**

*Data not provided

39 (cont'd) INTERNATIONAL SCHOLARS BY STATE, 1993/94 – 2003/04

Characteristic	PERCENT OF INTERNATIONAL SCHOLARS										
	1993/94	1994/95	1995/96	1996/97	1997/98	1998/99	1999/00	2000/01	2001/02	2002/03	2003/04
Visa Status											
J (All)	73.8	76.6	77.0	75.9	73.2	74.3	.	.	.	.	.
J-1	.	.	.	.	.	.	69.0	68.5	64.0	56.7	53.6
J-1 Other	.	.	.	.	.	.	2.6	2.3	2.7	3.7	2.5
H-1B	17.8	16.0	16.2	17.6	18.3	18.8	20.5	22.0	24.6	31.0	34.7
TN	.	.	.	.	.	.	1.5	1.6	1.6	1.3	2.3
O-1	.	.	.	.	.	.	0.8	1.1	1.2	1.1	0.9
Other	8.4	7.4	6.8	6.5	8.5	6.8	5.5	4.4	5.9	6.2	6.0
Sex											
Male	75.0	73.8	73.7	74.2	73.7	72.0	71.8	70.5	69.3	68.2	67.0
Female	25.0	26.2	26.3	25.8	26.3	28.0	28.2	29.5	30.7	31.8	33.0
Primary Function											
Research	79.8	80.7	82.6	81.9	83.1	81.0	76.5	79.2	77.2	74.2	75.8
Teaching	12.1	12.2	11.5	11.5	11.5	10.9	10.4	10.8	11.7	12.2	13.4
Both Research & Teaching	8.1	7.1	5.9	6.6	5.4	8.1	7.8	5.0	4.9	7.1	5.9
Other	.	.	.	.	.	.	5.3	5.0	6.2	6.5	5.0
TOTAL	**59,981**	**58,074**	**59,403**	**62,354**	**65,494**	**70,501**	**74,571**	**79,651**	**86,015**	**84,281**	**82,905**

40 VISA STATUS, SEX, AND PRIMARY FUNCTION OF INTERNATIONAL SCHOLARS, 1993/94 – 2003/04

Major Field of Specialization	PERCENT OF INTERNATIONAL SCHOLARS										
	1993/94	1994/95	1995/96	1996/97	1997/98	1998/99	1999/00	2000/01	2001/02	2002/03	2003/04
Life & Biological Sciences	13.1	14.1	12.8	15.4	14.4	15.4	16.8	14.7	14.6	17.5	23.2
Health Sciences	27.4	28.6	27.6	27.1	26.9	26.2	23.8	26.9	27.4	25.0	20.8
Physical Sciences	14.7	12.8	14.3	13.8	14.5	15.0	14.8	14.7	14.0	14.3	13.2
Engineering	11.6	11.9	13.4	11.8	11.7	12.6	11.9	12.6	11.4	11.8	10.7
Business & Management	3.2	2.8	2.9	2.6	2.5	2.3	2.4	2.5	3.1	2.9	3.8
Computer & Information Sciences	2.3	2.3	2.7	2.2	2.9	2.5	2.9	2.7	3.3	3.2	3.7
Social Sciences & History	4.6	4.0	4.2	4.6	4.6	4.3	3.9	3.6	4.5	4.1	3.3
Agriculture	3.7	3.4	3.5	4.1	4.0	3.4	3.6	3.9	3.4	3.9	3.1
Mathematics	2.9	2.5	2.8	2.8	2.9	2.8	2.6	2.5	2.6	2.7	2.4
Other	2.2	3.1	1.5	1.6	2.2	1.5	3.3	2.8	2.4	1.9	2.2
Foreign Languages & Literature	2.2	2.3	2.0	2.3	1.9	2.3	2.8	1.9	2.0	2.5	1.9
Education	1.5	1.8	1.6	1.4	1.4	1.4	1.4	1.5	1.5	1.6	1.6
Area & Ethnic Studies	1.7	1.8	1.5	1.6	1.7	1.8	1.8	1.8	1.4	1.4	1.5
Letters	1.5	1.4	1.7	1.8	1.6	1.5	1.4	1.3	1.4	1.1	1.4
Public Affairs	0.7	0.6	0.8	0.7	0.5	0.5	0.5	0.6	0.6	0.5	1.2
Psychology	0.9	0.9	0.9	0.8	1.0	1.0	1.1	1.0	1.0	1.0	1.2
Visual & Performing Arts	1.6	1.2	1.7	1.5	1.5	1.4	1.3	1.2	1.3	1.1	1.1
Law & Legal Studies	1.2	1.1	1.0	1.0	1.0	1.1	1.1	1.2	1.0	1.0	0.9
Philosophy & Religion	1.1	1.1	0.7	0.9	0.7	0.7	0.7	0.6	0.9	0.6	0.8
Communications	0.6	0.6	0.6	0.4	0.5	0.5	0.5	0.5	0.6	0.6	0.7
Architecture & Environmental Design	0.7	0.7	0.8	0.7	0.6	0.8	0.8	0.7	0.8	0.7	0.7
Home Economics	0.4	0.4	0.4	0.5	0.6	0.6	0.3	0.4	0.5	0.5	0.4
Library Sciences	0.3	0.2	0.2	0.3	0.3	0.3	0.3	0.3	0.3	0.3	0.3
Marketing	0.1	0.1	0.1	0.1	0.1	0.1	0.1	0.1	0.1	0.1	0.1
TOTAL	**59,981**	**58,074**	**59,403**	**62,354**	**65,494**	**70,501**	**74,571**	**79,651**	**86,015**	**84,281**	**82,905**

41 MAJOR FIELD OF SPECIALIZATION OF INTERNATIONAL SCHOLARS, 1993/94 – 2003/04

METHODOLOGY

ABOUT THE SURVEY

History of the Census

Since its founding in 1919, the Institute of International Education (IIE) has conducted an annual census of international students in the United States. For the first 30 years, IIE and the Committee on Friendly Relations Among Foreign Students carried out this effort jointly. IIE's first independent publication of the results of the annual census was *Education for One World*, containing data for the 1948/49 academic year. It was renamed the *Open Doors Report on International Educational Exchange* in 1954/55, and began receiving support from the Bureau of Educational and Cultural Affairs in USIA (now U.S. Department of State) in the early 1970s. *Open Doors* has long been regarded as the primary source for basic trends in international students, international scholars, and international students in Intensive English Programs in the U.S., as well as U.S. students studying abroad.

Country Classification System

The classification of places of origin into regional groupings that is used throughout this report is based on the U.S. Department of State's definitions of world regions and states [Table 42]. See *www.state.gov* for more information.

Code	Place of Origin
1000	AFRICA
1100	East Africa
1115	Burundi
1120	Comoros
1105	Djibouti
1195	Eritrea
1125	Ethiopia
1130	Kenya
1135	Madagascar
1140	Malawi
1145	Mauritius
1150	Mozambique
1155	Reunion
1165	Rwanda
1170	Seychelles
1175	Somalia
1180	Tanzania
1185	Uganda
1190	Zambia
1160	Zimbabwe
1200	Central Africa
1210	Angola
1220	Cameroon
1230	Central African Republic
1240	Chad
1250	Congo
1260	Equatorial Guinea
1270	Gabon
1280	São Tomé & Príncipe
1290	Congo/Zaire
1300	North Africa
1310	Algeria
1320	Canary Islands
1330	Egypt
1340	Libya
1350	Morocco
1370	Sudan
1380	Tunisia
1360	Western Sahara
1400	Southern Africa
1410	Botswana
1420	Lesotho
1430	Namibia
1440	South Africa
1450	Swaziland
1500	West Africa
1510	Benin
1585	Burkina Faso

Code	Place of Origin
1505	Cape Verde
1535	Côte d'Ivoire
1515	Gambia
1520	Ghana
1525	Guinea
1530	Guinea-Bissau
1540	Liberia
1545	Mali
1550	Mauritania
1555	Niger
1560	Nigeria
1565	St. Helena
1570	Senegal
1575	Sierra Leone
1580	Togo
2000	ASIA
2100	East Asia
2110	China
2120	Taiwan
2130	Hong Kong, China
2140	Japan
2150	Korea, Democratic People's Republic of
2160	Korea, Republic of
2170	Macao, China
2180	Mongolia
2200	South/Central Asia
2205	Afghanistan
2210	Bangladesh
2215	Bhutan
2220	India
2260	Kazakhstan
2265	Kyrgyzstan
2225	Maldives, Republic of
2230	Nepal
2235	Pakistan
2245	Sri Lanka
2270	Tajikistan
2250	Turkmenistan
2255	Uzbekistan
2300	Southeast Asia
2305	Brunei
2320	Cambodia
2315	Indonesia
2325	Laos
2330	Malaysia
2310	Myanmar

42 PLACE OF ORIGIN CODES BY PLACE OF ORIGIN WITHIN WORLD REGION

2335	Philippines		3263	Monaco
2345	Singapore		3266	Netherlands
2350	Thailand		3270	Norway
2360	Vietnam		3273	Portugal
2370	East Timor		3276	San Marino
			3280	Spain
3000	EUROPE		3283	Sweden
3100	Eastern Europe		3286	Switzerland
3110	Albania		3290	United Kingdom
3189	Armenia		3240	Vatican City
3174	Azerbaijan			
3181	Belarus		4000	LATIN AMERICA
3193	Bosnia & Herzegovina		4100	Caribbean
3120	Bulgaria		4103	Aruba
3191	Croatia		4105	Bahamas
3131	Czech Republic		4110	Barbados
3130	Czechoslovakia, Former		4115	Cayman Islands
3183	Estonia		4120	Cuba
3188	Georgia		4125	Dominican Republic
3150	Hungary		4130	Guadeloupe
3184	Latvia		4135	Haiti
3185	Lithuania		4140	Jamaica
3194	Macedonia		4150	Leeward Islands
3187	Moldova		4155	Anguilla
3160	Poland		4151	Antigua
3170	Romania		4152	British Virgin Islands
3186	Russia		4153	Montserrat
3132	Slovakia		4154	St. Kitts-Nevis
3192	Slovenia		4160	Martinique
3182	Ukraine		4170	Netherlands Antilles
3180	U.S.S.R., Former		4180	Trinidad & Tobago
3190	Yugoslavia, Former		4185	Turks & Caicos Isles
3200	Western Europe		4190	Windward Islands
3203	Andorra		4191	Dominica
3206	Austria		4192	Grenada
3210	Belgium		4193	St. Lucia
3213	Denmark		4194	St. Vincent
3220	Finland		4200	Central America/Mexico
3223	France		4210	Belize
3226	Germany		4230	Costa Rica
3233	Gibraltar		4240	El Salvador
3236	Greece		4250	Guatemala
3243	Iceland		4260	Honduras
3246	Ireland		4270	Mexico
3250	Italy		4280	Nicaragua
3253	Liechtenstein		4290	Panama
3256	Luxembourg		4300	South America
3260	Malta			

42 (cont'd) PLACE OF ORIGIN CODES BY PLACE OF ORIGIN WITHIN WORLD REGION

Fields of Study

The fields of study used in this book are from the *Classification of Instructional Programs, 2000*, published by the National Center for Education Statistics (NCES) of the U.S. Department of Education. For more information about the codes, see *www.nces.ed.gov/pubs2002/cip2000*. See Table 43 for a list of major fields of study.

Carnegie Classification System

Open Doors 2004 uses the 2000 Carnegie classifications, or codes.[1] Prior editions of *Open Doors* used the 1994 Carnegie codes. In the change from the 1994 to the 2000 editions of the codes, the Carnegie Classification system changed some institutions' codes, and some of the categories themselves were revised. Because *Open Doors* uses the Carnegie system for its rankings, as well as for various analyses, comparisons to previous years' *Open Doors* cannot readily be made. See *www.carnegiefoundation.org/classification* for a fuller discussion about the Carnegie Classification system.

About the Annual Census of International Students

For the purposes of the Census, an international student is defined as an individual who is enrolled for courses at a higher education institution in the U.S. on a temporary visa, and who is not an immigrant (permanent resident

1 Carnegie Foundation for the Advancement of Teaching, The Carnegie Classifications of Institutions of Higher Education, 2000 Edition. Electronic Data File, Fourth Revision, 2003.

with an I-151 or "Green Card"), a citizen, an illegal alien (undocumented immigrant), or a refugee. The data presented in *Open Doors 2004* were obtained through a survey conducted, in Fall 2003 through Spring 2004, of campus officials at 2,685 regionally accredited institutions of higher education in the U.S. Of the institutions surveyed, 2,345 or 87.3% responded to the questionnaire [Table 44]. The response rate, although always high, has fluctuated over the history of the Census, reaching the lowest point in the mid-1970s. However, in the past decade it has been very high, ranging from 92.6% in 1979/80 to 99.5% in 1987/88. The high response rates are the product of extensive e-mail and telephone follow-ups, in addition to four mail follow-ups.

Almost 95% (2,225) of the responding institutions reported enrolling international students [Table 44]. Of the schools with international students, a total of 281 (13%) provided only total international student counts (Step 1) [Table 45]. The majority (87%), however, provided information not only on the total but also on the students' place of origin, field of study, academic level, sex, and other characteristics (Step 2). The Step 2 response rate is the highest in three years, resulting in more comprehensive and better quality data. The vast majority of the institutions with international students provided data on some or all of the student characteristics [Table 46]. Some variables commanded a greater number of responses

4305	Argentina		2485	Yemen
4310	Bolivia			
4315	Brazil		**5000**	**NORTH AMERICA**
4320	Chile		5110	Bermuda
4325	Colombia		5120	Canada
4330	Ecuador			
4335	Falkland Islands		**6000**	**OCEANIA**
4340	French Guiana		**6100**	**Australia/New Zealand**
4345	Guyana		6110	Australia
4350	Paraguay		6120	New Zealand
4355	Peru		**6200**	**Pacific Ocean Island Areas**
4360	Suriname		6210	Cook Islands
4365	Uruguay		6215	Fiji
4370	Venezuela		6220	French Polynesia
			6225	Kiribati
2400	**MIDDLE EAST**		6227	Marshall Islands
2405	Bahrain		6260	Micronesia, Federated States of
2410	Cyprus			
2415	Iran		6230	Nauru
2420	Iraq		6235	New Caledonia
2425	Israel		6250	Niue
2430	Jordan		6255	Norfolk Island
2435	Kuwait		6263	Palau
2440	Lebanon		6240	Papua New Guinea
2445	Oman		6205	Solomon Islands
2443	Palestinian Authority		6270	Tonga
2450	Qatar		6271	Tuvalu
2455	Saudi Arabia		6245	Vanuatu
2460	Syria		6275	Wallis & Futuna Isles
2465	Turkey		6280	Western Samoa
2470	United Arab Emirates			
			7000	**ANTARCTICA**

42 **(cont'd) PLACE OF ORIGIN CODES BY PLACE OF ORIGIN WITHIN WORLD REGION**

AGRICULTURE
01   Agriculture, Agriculture Operations, and Related Sciences
03   Conservation and Renewable Natural Resources

ARCHITECTURE AND RELATED PROGRAMS
04   Architecture and Related Services

AREA, ETHNIC, CULTURAL, AND GENDER STUDIES
05   Area, Ethnic, Cultural, and Gender Studies

BUSINESS MANAGEMENT AND ADMINISTRATIVE SERVICES
8   Marketing Operations/Marketing and Distribution
52   Business, Management, Marketing, and Related Support Services

43 **FIELD OF STUDY CATEGORY CODES**

COMMUNICATIONS
9   Communications, Journalism, and Related Programs
10   Communication Technologies/Technicians and Support Services

COMPUTER AND INFORMATION SCIENCES
11   Computer and Information Sciences and Support Services

PERSONAL AND CULINARY SERVICES
12   Personal and Culinary Services

EDUCATION
13   Education

ENGINEERING
14   Engineering
15   Engineering Technologies/Technicians

FOREIGN LANGUAGES AND LITERATURE
16   Foreign Languages, Literature, and Linguistics

HEALTH
51   Health Professions and Related Clinical Services

HOME ECONOMICS
19   Family and Consumer Sciences/Human Sciences
20   Vocational Home Economics

LAW AND LEGAL STUDIES
22   Legal Profession and Studies

ENGLISH LANGUAGE AND LITERATURE/LETTERS
23   English Language and Literature/Letters

LIBERAL/GENERAL STUDIES
24   Liberal Arts and Sciences, General Studies, and Humanities

LIBRARY SCIENCES
25   Library Sciences

LIFE SCIENCES
26   Biological and Biomedical Sciences

MATHEMATICS
27   Mathematics and Statistics

MILITARY TECHNOLOGIES
28   R.O.T.C. (Reserve Officer Training Corps)
29   Military Technologies

MULTI/INTERDISCIPLINARY STUDIES
30   Multi/Interdisciplinary Studies

PARKS, RECREATION, LEISURE, AND FITNESS STUDIES
31   Parks, Recreation, and Fitness Studies

43   (cont'd) FIELD OF STUDY CATEGORY CODES

than others. Data on academic level were provided for over 90%, and place of origin breakdowns for almost 88%. Conversely, information on the students' primary source of funding and on their marital status was available for less than half of the total number reported (approximately 43% and 41%, respectively).

About the International Scholar Survey

For the purposes of this survey, international scholars are defined as non-immigrant, non-student academics (teachers and/or researchers, administrators) in the U.S. Scholars may also be affiliated with U.S. institutions for other activities such as conferences, colloquia, observations, consultations, or other short-term professional development activities. The survey was limited to doctoral degree-granting institutions where most J Visa scholars were based. This survey, which was conducted online, captured scholar-related information for the period beginning on July 1, 2003 and ending June 30, 2004. Institutions were asked about the primary function of the scholars (research, teaching, both, or other), their geographic origin, field of specialization, sex, and immigration/visa status. Responses were received from 221 of the 353 institutions polled, for a response rate of 62.6%. Based on the past practice of estimating for non-response for this survey [see below, "Imputation and Estimation"], data from 41 additional institutions (overall totals only) were included, and thus 74.2% of the institutions were represented in the analysis. Most institutions reporting international scholars in 2003/04 were able to provide detailed information on the characteristics of their scholars, and the response rates for the various survey items far exceeded those seen in years' past [Table 47]. The proportion of institutions that provided breakdowns for individual variables ranged from almost 90% for visa status and sex to almost 69% for field of specialization.

About the U.S. Study Abroad Survey

This survey focuses on study abroad for academic credit. The study abroad population is defined as only those students (U.S. citizens and permanent residents) enrolled for a degree at a U.S. accredited higher education institution who received academic credit for study abroad from their home institution upon their return. Students studying abroad without credit are not included here, nor are U.S. students enrolled overseas for degrees. The number of students who receive academic credit is inevitably lower than the number of all students who go abroad. Hence, the figures presented here give a conservative picture of study abroad activity.

Study abroad information was obtained from 1,022 or 78.4% of the 1,303 surveyed institutions for the 2002/03 academic year, including summer 2003. While lower than last year's rate of

PHILOSOPHY AND RELIGIOUS STUDIES	
38	Philosophy
39	Theological Studies and Religious Vocations
PHYSICAL SCIENCES	
40	Physical Sciences
41	Science Technologies/Technicians
PSYCHOLOGY	
42	Psychology
SECURITY AND PROTECTIVE SERVICES	
43	Protective Services
PUBLIC ADMINISTRATION AND SOCIAL SERVICE PROFESSIONS	
44	Public Administration and Services
SOCIAL SCIENCES AND HISTORY	
45	Social Sciences
54	History
TRADE AND INDUSTRIAL	
46	Construction Trades
47	Mechanics and Repairs
48	Precision Production
49	Transportation and Material Moving
VISUAL AND PERFORMING ARTS	
50	Visual and Performing Arts
RESIDENCY PROGRAMS	
60	Residency Programs
UNDECLARED	
90	Undeclared
INTENSIVE ENGLISH	
99**	Intensive English

* Source: National Center for Education Statistics, Classification of Instructional Programs, 2000 (Washington, D.C.: NCES, 2001). Web address: nces.ed.gov/pubs2002/cip2000.

** Code created to capture Intensive English, which is not represented among the CIP 2000 codes

43 **(cont'd) FIELD OF STUDY CATEGORY CODES**

87.1%, it nonetheless represents a substantial response resulting from repeated requests for data. This included three follow-ups sent via mail, phone and e-mail follow-ups, as well as the assistance the SECUSSA Data Collection Committee of NAFSA provides each year in urging institutions to respond.

The survey included an item on internships and work abroad, and was amended in the current year to better capture financial aid for study abroad, as well as the study abroad experience among community college students. Not all institutions provided detailed information about the characteristics of the students [Table 48]. The proportion of

Year	Institutions Surveyed	Institutions w/ Int'l Students	Institutions w/o Int'l Students	Total Responding Institutions	% Response
1964/65	2,556	1,859	434	2,293	89.7
1969/70	2,859	1,734	265	1,999	69.9
1974/75	3,085	1,760	148	1,908	61.8
1979/80	3,186	2,651	299	2,950	92.6
1984/85	2,833	2,492	274	2,766	97.6
1989/90	2,891	2,546	294	2,840	98.2
1990/91	2,879	2,543	241	2,784	96.7
1991/92	2,823	2,436	228	2,646	94.4
1992/93	2,783	2,417	166	2,583	92.8
1993/94	2,743	2,451	163	2,614	95.3
1994/95	2,758	2,517	167	2,684	97.3
1995/96	2,715	2,403	176	2,579	95.7
1996/97	2,732	2,428	185	2,613	95.6
1997/98	2,726	2,394	177	2,571	94.3
1998/99	2,708	2,446	142	2,588	95.6
1999/00	2,696	2,367	126	2,493	92.5
2000/01	2,699	2,344	120	2,464	91.3
2001/02	2,697	2,284	100	2,384	88.4
2002/03	2,697	2,307	113	2,420	90.0
2003/04	2,685	2,225	118	2,345	87.3

44   INSTITUTIONS SURVEYED AND TYPE OF RESPONSE, SELECTED YEARS 1964/65 – 2003/04

Type of Response	2001/02 Number	%	2002/03 Number	%	2003/04 Number	%
Total Only - STEP 1	422	20.7	445	17.7	281	12.6
Institutional Data - STEP 2	1,962	79.3	1,862	82.3	1,944	87.4
Total with Students	**2,384**		**2,307**		**2,225**	

45   INSTITUTIONS REPORTING INTERNATIONAL STUDENTS AND TYPE OF RESPONSE, 2001/02 – 2003/04

dividing the total number of undergraduates in study abroad in a given year by the total number of undergraduate completions.[2] This is a proxy estimate of the proportion of students in a two-or four-year cohort who go through a study abroad experience at least once during their academic career.

About the Intensive English Program Survey

IIE and two leading professional Intensive English Program (IEP) associations, the American Association of Intensive English Language Programs (AAIEP) and the University and College Intensive English Programs (UCIEP), collaborated to collect national data that reflect IEP activity in the U.S. Data elements in this survey include program sponsorship, the percentage of students intending to continue further (non-IEP) study in the U.S., program duration (18 hours or more, 18 hours or less), and place of origin. Student totals reflect both headcount enrollment and enrollment by "student-weeks." One student-week equals one student studying for one week.

The number of institutions invited to participate also included non-AAIEP and UCIEP institutions. These IEPs were taken from IIE's *Intensive English USA (IEUSA) 2000* directory. In all, 525

schools that gave breakdowns for individual variables ranged from slightly over 55% for field of study to over 86% for host country or destination.

Participation rates: In collaboration with the study abroad community, IIE began the practice of reporting undergraduate completion rates, by using undergraduate completions (graduations) data. These undergraduate participation calculations use Integrated Postsecondary Education Data System (IPEDS) data, which are produced by the U.S. Department of Education [*http://nces.ed.gov/ipeds*]. After the IPEDS and study abroad survey files are matched, participation is calculated by

2 Although the IPEDS data are sometimes lagged a year, completion data are usually stable enough for this purpose.

programs were contacted by e-mail (315 AAIEP & UCIEP programs and 210 non-members) and returns were obtained from 181 programs for an over-all response rate of 34.5%. The 43,003 students reported this year represents student enrollments throughout the 2003 calendar year (January 1, 2003 to December 31, 2003). The mix of report-ing institutions reflects university and college-affiliated programs as well as large for-profit entities that offer English language training. As with our other sur-veys, not all programs pro-viding total numbers could provide detailed breakouts of duration of study by number of students (72.4% of stu-dents), duration of study in student-weeks (72.4% of programs), and the percent of students pursuing further study (65.7% of programs) [Table 49].

Imputation and Estimation

Category	Base Number	% of Int'l Students
Academic Level	520,285	90.9
Field of Study	502,923	87.8
Sex	494,680	86.4
Place of Origin	483,665	84.5
Enrollment Status	455,105	79.5
Visa (Immigration) Status	450,867	78.8
Primary Source of Funds	248,113	43.3
Marital Status	231,850	40.5
Total Reported	**572,509**	

46 INSTITUTIONS REPORTING INTERNATIONAL STUDENTS BY INDIVIDUAL VARIABLES, 2003/04

	1995/96 %	1996/97 %	1997/98 %	1998/99 %	1999/00 %	2000/01 %	2001/02 %	2002/03 %	2003/04 %
Visa Status	90.8	92.9	84.2	94.8	70.4	85.5	76.7	66.1	89.6
Place of Origin	88.3	90.8	83.6	88.9	94.5	82.3	71.7	63.6	77.4
Sex	81.3	88.3	80.2	82.9	64.8	79.4	70.8	58.0	89.6
Primary Function	77.1	88.2	69.2	81.9	67.7	76.9	70.3	57.4	78.3
Field of Specialization	85.9	88.4	84.0	87.8	65.9	78.9	67.3	56.1	68.8
Total	**59,403**	**62,354**	**65,494**	**70,501**	**74,571**	**79,651**	**86,015**	**84,281**	**82,905**

47 RESPONSE RATE TO INDIVIDUAL VARIABLES: INTERNATIONAL SCHOLAR SURVEY, 1995/96 – 2003/04

Throughout this document, total inter-national student enrollments, U.S. study abroad totals, international scholar totals, IEP totals, and the various per-centages herein are calculated directly from campus-based survey responses. Other student counts are determined by imputation, since not all campuses are able to provide detailed breakdowns by the various categories, such as place of origin, field of study, etc. Estimates of the number of students for each of the vari-ables collected by the various surveys are imputed from the total number of stu-dents reported. For each imputation, base or raw counts are multiplied by a correction factor that reflects the ratio of difference between the sum of the cate-gories being imputed and the total num-ber of students reported by institutions. For this reason, student totals may vary slightly within this publication. In addi-tion, due to rounding, percentages do not always add up to 100% (whether or not numbers are imputed).

The data collection methodology was designed to produce stable, national estimates of international education activity. Analysis for units that reflect relatively small numbers of students (certain nationalities, fields of study, sources of financial support) and espe-cially those that are cut by other vari-ables may reflect greater error variation than variables with a larger response base. In addition, to account for poten-tial instability in annual institution-level counts, estimates based on counts

Category	1993/94 %	1994/95 %	1995/96 %	1996/97 %	1997/98 %	1998/99 %	1999/00 %	2000/01 %	2001/02 %	2002/03 %
Duration of Study	93.1	77.7	91.2	89.8	85.9	89.5	92.5	92.1	93.0	69.9
Host Destination	91.3	79.5	91.0	88.4	80.6	86.3	92.2	91.4	91.0	86.3
Program Sponsorship	90.7	73.8	92.2	88.7	86.2	87.2	91.0	89.6	90.0	67.4
Academic Level	80.1	63.6	77.8	78.5	78.1	79.2	82.1	83.1	80.2	62.2
Sex	80.3	65.6	76.1	75.1	75.9	76.3	81.0	80.3	80.2	78.2
Field of Study	64.3	45.9	60.2	62.8	65.1	65.6	75.1	80.5	77.6	55.3
Race/Ethnicity	43.3	33.0	39.7	40.9	42.6	44.8	45.7	50.3	47.7	57.2
Students Reported	**76,302**	**84,403**	**89,242**	**99,448**	**113,959**	**129,770**	**143,590**	**154,168**	**160,920**	**174,629**

48   RESPONSE RATE TO INDIVIDUAL VARIABLES: STUDY ABROAD SURVEY, 1993/94 – 2002/03

Category	# of Reporting Programs	% of All Participating Programs
Total Number of Students	181	100.0
Program Type	181	100.0
Total Number of Student-Weeks	181	100.0
Number of Students by Place of Origin	181	100.0
Number of Student-Weeks by Place of Origin	181	100.0
Duration of Study, Number of Students	131	72.4
Duration of Study, Number of Student-Weeks	131	72.4
Percent of Students Pursuing Further Study	119	65.7

49   RESPONSE RATE TO INDIVIDUAL VARIABLES: INTENSIVE ENGLISH PROGRAM SURVEY, 2003

from the previous reporting year (if available) are sometimes used to account for any given non-reporting institution, but if and only if there is a history of reporting to *Open Doors* surveys and the previous year's figures were not themselves so estimated. For International Students and Study Abroad, these estimates are based upon the prior year's number adjusted by the average percent change among institutions that reported in the prior and current academic years. For International

Scholars counts, estimates to account for non-reporting campuses were based on numbers reported in the previous year (if available and not estimated itself), with no additional adjustment. The only case where estimation was not performed was for Intensive English: unlike the other survey data presented in this current volume, and in a departure from prior years, no estimates were produced to account for IEP non-reporting due to changes in the data collection and analysis procedures. While estimation refine-

ments were made for this edition and will continue to be made for future editions, the general practice of estimating based on previous years' numbers is entirely consistent with past years' *Open Doors* analysis protocols.

Differences exist between the sum of undergraduate/graduate breakdowns by place of origin [Table 2] and the "official" aggregate undergraduate/graduate totals [Table 18]. The official figure is based on data from each reporting U.S. institution of their total enrollment of international students by academic level. While most institutions report academic level breakdowns by place of origin, others are unable to do so. The data shown in Table 2 are adjusted only to the extent to which institutions are able to provide academic level data by place of origin. In practice, *Open Doors* does not adjust further for this discrepancy, and uses the overall academic level, not the academic level by nationality, as the basis for calculating changes from year to year and for analyses.

ACKNOWLEDGMENTS

Producing the *Open Doors Report* involves the cooperation and contributions of many individuals and organizations. The Bureau of Educational and Cultural Affairs of the U.S. Department of State has provided funding to the Institute since the 1970s. This grant enables the Institute to collect, analyze, publish, and disseminate the data on international students, U.S. students abroad, and international scholars. The American Association of Intensive English Programs (AAIEP) and University and College Intensive English Programs in the USA (UCIEP), two leading Intensive English Language Program organizations, have provided the Institute support since 1999 to collect and report data on international students in Intensive English Programs in the U.S.

Each year AACRAO, the American Association of Collegiate Registrars and Admissions Officers, College Board, Council of Graduate Schools, and NAFSA: Association of International Educators, support and advise the Institute on *Open Doors* in their role as representatives of the field. Kim Kreutzer, Chair, and the SECUSSA Data Collection Committee of NAFSA worked with the Institute to continue to improve reporting among study abroad data providers. Don Back, Vice-President for Advocacy at AAIEP and District Director of ELS Language Centers in St. Petersburg, FL assisted in publicizing the IEP survey to AAIEP and UCIEP members, and in encouraging responses. Lynn Schoch and Jason Baumgartner of Indiana University at Bloomington analyzed the economic impact of international students in the U.S.

Without the contributions of colleagues at institutions who provided data, especially those who do so consistently each year, *Open Doors* would not be the comprehensive, reliable data source that it is.

Many individuals outside of the Institute assisted in the production process. Gilbert Jyoung and Laura Koo worked to ensure that the data was as accurate as possible. Lenora Komlacevs at Automated Data Solutions oversaw the data entry. Renée Meyer, of Renée Meyer Graphics, designed the finished product that you see. Lori Gilbert and Alan Flint at Automated Graphic Systems assisted us through the printing process.

At the Institute, Peggy Blumenthal, Vice-President for Educational Services, oversees the entire project. Sharon Witherell, assisted by Hannah Thompson at the Institute and Debbie Gardner and Heidi Reinholdt at Halstead Communications, the Institute's public relations firm, is instrumental in disseminating the report to a wider audience beyond the field. Daniel Obst, assisted by Toby Rugger, maintains the *Open Doors* site on IIENetwork. This year, Dr. Adria Gallup-Black, Director of Research & Evaluation at IIE, analyzed the data and prepared some of the text.

We at the Institute hope that *Open Doors* continues to serve as a comprehensive and reliable information resource to those in the field of international education, as well as to others outside the field who have an interest in international exchanges.

Hey-Kyung Koh Chin
Editor, *Open Doors*
Institute of International Education

New York City
December 2004